2-13-06

# TIMOTHY

# . . TIMOTHY

or, Notes of an Abject Reptile

Verlyn Klinkenborg

 Alfred A. Knopf • New York • 2006

THIS IS A BORZOI BOOK
PUBLISHED BY ALFRED A. KNOPF

www.aaknopf.com

Knopf, Borzoi Books, and the colophon are registered trademarks
of Random House, Inc.

Library of Congress Cataloging-in-Publication Data

Klinkenborg, Verlyn.
Timothy, or, Notes of an abject reptile / by Verlyn Klinkenborg.
        p. cm.
    ISBN 0-679-40728-6
    1. Turtles—Fiction. 2. Naturalists—Fiction. 3. Selborne (England)—
Fiction. 4. Human-animal relationships—Fiction. 5. White, Gilbert,
1720–1793—Fiction. I. Title: Notes of an abject reptile. II. Title.

PS3611.L565T55 2006
813'6—dc22        2005048779

Printed in the United States of America
First Edition

*To Lindy*

# TIMOTHY

A very intelligent and observant person has assured me that, in the former part of his life, keeping but one horse, he happened also on a time to have but one solitary hen. These two incongruous animals spent much of their time together in a lonely orchard, where they saw no creature but each other. By degrees an apparent regard began to take place between these two sequestered individuals. The fowl would approach the quadruped with notes of complacency, rubbing herself gently against his legs: while the horse would look down with satisfaction, and move with the greatest caution and circumspection, lest he should trample on his diminutive companion. Thus, by mutual good offices, each seemed to console the vacant hours of the other: so that *Milton*, when he puts the following sentiment in the mouth of *Adam*, seems to be somewhat mistaken:

> *Much less can bird with beast, or fish with fowl,*
> *So well converse, nor with the ox the ape.*

Gilbert White, *The Natural History of Selborne*, 1789.

The way to Selborne is *Dorchester*, *Wallingford*, *Pangborn*; here leave the Reading-road, and go down the new turn-pike for *Aldermaston*-wharf, *Aldermaston*; *Basingstoke*, *Tunworth-down*, under *Hackwood*-park pales, the *Golden-pot* ale-house, *Alton*, *Faringdon*, *Horse-and-Jockey*, *Selborne*.

Gilbert White to Ralph Churton, 31 August 1780.

I was gone for more than a week before they found me. A rustling in the bean-field, heavy steps nearby. A shout—the boy's voice—more shouts. Thomas catches me up in his hands with sickening haste. I weigh six pounds thirteen ounces. He lifts me as though I weigh nothing at all.

Ground breaks away. May wind shivers in my ears. My legs churn the sky on their own. I look down on bean-tops. Down on the blunt ends of sheep-bitten grasses. Over one field, into the next, into the hop-garden beyond. Past thatch and tiles, past maypole, past gilded cock on the church tower. All in my eye, all at once. So far to see.

Goody Hammond and Daniel Wheeler's boy totter forward beside Thomas. Great warm two-legged beasts. Stilt-gaited like the rest of their kind. The boy prances backward, eyeing me closely. Bland watery orbs, fringed with pale hair. Cavernous mouth. Halloos as though I were the king's stag being drawn through the village in a deer-cart.

# Timothy

My week gone in two-score of their strides. Through the meadow. Past the alcove and down the brick-walk. Wicket-gate clicks shut behind us. Thomas sets me down beside the asparagus. Edge of my umbrageous forest. All feet square on the ground again. Into the rubbery trunks. Young asparagus thrusting out of the earth like turtles' heads. Ferns just joining in a canopy above. Print of Thomas's warm fingers on my tiled belly, smell of tar and damp mould.

The voices separate and blow away. The boy's cries ring down the street with cries of other boys. A silence behind them, a hollow in the day. Earthworms breach and tunnel, tunnel and breach. Old Hercules in the Great Mead gestures as always, unmoving. Wooden features sadly weathered even since I first knew him. Goody Hammond sweeps white-apple blossoms from the grass-plot. Sings a scrap of song over and over as she works. Wheezing like the blacksmith's bellows across the way.

"O Christ! My very Heart doth bleed with Sorrow for thy Sake . . ."

Greenfinch rattles in the beds nearby, heedless of danger. Mayfly vanishes in the blur of a swallow's wings over the gravel walk. Swallow-bill closes, a smart snap, shutting of a watch-case.

The fuss the humans made when they found me. Escape of the Old Sussex Tortoise! Eight Days' Pursuit! Captured in Hampshire Bean-field! Authentic Deeds of Old Gardener, Weeding Woman, Shocking Boy!

Thomas regarded me sternly before setting me down. Cocked his hat. Took breath to speak, then didn't. Watched till I was deep in the asparagus, safely out of sight.

"Out!" Daniel Wheeler's boy shouted when they found me, stumbling over his heels. "Timothy got out!"

The boy is mistaken. There is no O*ut*! Humans believe the asparagus forest is I*n*! Fruit wall, laurel hedge. Melon-ground. They prey upon the distinction. But I am always O*ut*. Among the anemones. On the grass-plot. In the shade of the Dutch-currant trees. In the sainfoin just short of the Pound Field. Under young beans a week away. Under the rasp and green-rust smell of their leaves.

And I was I*n* there, too, as always. In, under unhedged stars, dark of the moon. Among chiding of field-crickets, stirring of long grasses, gleaming wind. Groaning of beech trees on the Hanger. Clap of thunder and din of hail. The honeyed smell of maples and sycamores in bloom. Clouds pulling apart to show their crimson. Beyond sight of humans. Within my beloved shell.

Great soft tottering beasts. *They* are *out*. Houses never by when they need them. Even the humblest villagers live in ill-fitting houses. The greater the personage the worse the fit. Crescent of pale shell at the ends of their fingers. Drab furrows of person-scented cloth hang about them. Dimity, corduroy, buckram, fustian, holland, shalloon, cambric, stuff, wool. False head of hair or kerchief or hat.

Contrivance of hide or wood on the feet, or none at all. Crust of polished dirt, sore-cracked soles, broken nails.

# Timothy

Nothing as elegant as a horse's clean hoof, the arc of its wall. My own cruel claws. That mass of body and brainpan to heat and cool with their internal fires. No tegument, no pelt to help them. Only what they fashion for themselves. What they scab together from the world. Fleece, hide, feathers, scales, and shell all denied them. Faint, thin leather of their own growing, proof against nothing. Uneconomic creatures.

Humans of Selborne wake all winter. Above ground, eating and eating, breathing and shitting, talking and talking. Huddled close to their fires. Fanning the ashes. Guarding the spark. Never a lasting silence for them. Never more than a one-night rest. When they go down in the ground, they go down in boxes, for good, and only with the help of others standing round. Peering into the darkness of the cold earth they fear. The neat, rectangular hole.

Men haul peat from the forest, laboring over ruts and horse-tracks and onto the village cart-way. They measure out bushels of coal. Cut cord-wood. Stack beech-billet, cleft-wood, and faggots. Go to law over lop and top. Smoke beats down over the village. Tumbles from chimneys, thick over the fields. Beech-smoke, coal-smoke, peat-smoke. London smoke, a sulfurous haze from the northeast.

Cold wind settles against the glass. Rain under the tiles, through the wind-torn thatch. Only the oak-shingled roof of St. Mary's keeps tight above the village. Flights of snow. Epidemic freeze. Winter comes like the clamoring of the stone-curlew. A noise in the air of something passing quick over their heads after it becomes dark.

To humans, in and out are matters of life and death. Not to me. Warm earth waits just beneath me, the planet's viscous, scalding core. It takes a cool blood to feel that warmth, here at its circumference. The humans' own heat keeps them from sensing it. I drift for months—year's great night—floating on the outer edge of Earth's corona. The only calendar my blood, how it drugs me.

When autumn pinches, I dig. November darkens, fasting long since begun. Day after day. Steady, steady. Stroke on one side. Stroke on the other. Slow as the hour-hand and just as relentless. Swimming in place, burrowing my body's length and depth. Ease in, out, adjust the fit. Another day or two. No rush. No rush. Ease in again. A last fitting. Air hole open. Stow legs. Retreat under roof of self. Under vault of ribs and spine.

Loose earth covers my back. Laurel leaves, walnut leaves, chalk soil, Dorton mould. I wait, then cease to wait. Earth rolls repeatedly through day and night. Layer of rime. The frost binds. Then snow, that friendly meteor. Kindly mantle of infant vegetation. Insulating all of us who cling to the soil. Who have not got too upright, too far from the native horizontal. Earth beneath me throbs with warmth. Cold black sky presses down. Current of memory tugs at me. A long, long descent into perfect absence. I remember only where I'm going.

# Timothy

· · · · · ⌣

**M**eanwhile, the village stirs. Boys slide on ice. Girls chap hands. Straddle-bob Orion tips downward over the brew-house, over the Hanger. Barnyard turnip-piles freeze hard as stone. Men shovel the track to Newton. Hollow lanes— deep as a cottage, narrow as a walk—fill with snow. Pack-horses go belly-deep in open country.

Rugged Siberian weather. Laplandian-scene. The village cut off for weeks, hidden in the folds of England. Poultry confounded. Bantams fly over their house. Forty-one sheep buried in snow. Redbreasts, wrens, and beggars in barns and cow-houses. Worries about prices of mutton, hay, bar-ley seed. Haws freeze on hedges. Pheasant stands on dung-pile. Hares cross the garden snowpack and crop the pinks. Gardeners take aim from the windows.

Mr. Gilbert White watches through the parlor window. Tries to remember just where he saw me digging last fall. All his garden buried in drifts. Returns to his letter. Stitch in his side from writing. To niece Molly in London, asking her to send breakfast green tea and best tea. Great beast of a town. Cold as Petersburg. Londoners on the frozen Thames. Snow like bay-salt. Carriages quiet on the cobbles for once, cushioned by snow. Sound of a deserted city. Many weeks until mackerels are cried in the streets. Until green geese move along them in droves, driven by a boy just their speed.

Mr. Gilbert White writes. Mad dog from Newton great farm bites dogs in the Selborne street. Farmer Berriman's cow, he reports, "got into the barn's floor in the night, and gorged herself so at an heap of thrashed wheat, that she dyed what they call *sprung*, being blown up to a vast size." Seventeen residents of Newton farm, and a horse, have gone in a cart to be dipped in the sea. Mrs. John White knits beside Mr. Gilbert White. One row for her old life, one for the new.

Parlor-cat turns electric in dry nights of frost. Parlor-fire rages. Close-stools freeze beneath beds. Horses breathe their stable-fog. Lambs drop from the womb and freeze to the ground. Venus shadows. Walls stream with water. Thatch reeks in the sun. Fields pour torrents into the lanes that worm their way toward Selborne. Waking dreams of the human winter.

My blood creeps along a dark endless track. On quiet feet. Circles round and round as though it had lost its way but always finding its way again. No counting the circuits it makes under the compass-rose of my carapace.

One day corpuscles prick as they pass. Agitation in the capillaries. New trails through the underwood of flesh. Fresh tide washes over the rocks. Rushing millstream spills through the heart. I rouse before I know I'm rousing. Hatched from the great egg of Earth. Spring-wrecked on the surface, my living to make. Pipped again.

I blink and blink. Look into my crater, the nest that bears

me over and over and over and over. Surprised to come up always just where I went down. To be the only hatchling. Surprised to find myself in the parish of Selborne, county of Southampton, garden of Mr. Gilbert White.

I remember Ringmer. Mrs. Rebecca Snooke. A post-chaise. A servant's basket. A ship. The empty city of my origins, far away. Warm salt sea spreading at its feet. Cyprus in the distance. Nike and Hermes in mosaics underfoot. As weathered as old Hercules but far more ancient. A country swollen with emptiness and heat. I once had other expectations.

⌒ • • • • •

I heave up the mould. Unbury myself. In this place, I am considered a sign of spring, like the budding of beeches on the Hanger or the return of the first birds of passage. But I am a sign of spring the way flooding in Gracious Street is a sign of high water. Over the goose-hatch. The thing itself. The season advances directly through me.

Year after year Mr. Gilbert White notes the occasion. He has been up for months. Stands over me while rising still blinds me, before hunger returns. Long winter lingering in mouth and bowel. Mr. Gilbert White records the date, the weather. Conjunction, at my arrival, of a bat, a redstart, a daffodil, a troop of shell-snails.

"Timothy the tortoise begins to stir," he writes; "he heaves up the mould that lies over his back."

"Timothy the tortoise heaves up the sod under which he is buried."

"Timothy the tortoise heaves-up the earth."

"Timothy the tortoise roused himself from his winter-slumbers and came forth."

No other news in Selborne? No mad dog a-biting? No cow a-springing on a barn floor? What makes my rising momentous to anyone but me?

I have seen these humans in their disarray. Far more common than any finery. Hair wrung into knots. Stockings fallen. Skirts clotted with mud and manure. Eyes, noses red from fist-rubbings, coarsening wind. Eruptions on rough hands from hop-picking. Itching tumors from harvest-bugs. Jaws tied up with the tooth-ache, the head-ache. Faces choked with drink, sweat, sleep, stupidity, confusions of the rut. Such a bulk of being to regulate. Disorder stalks them day and night. They stalk it back.

But I. Consider that I have no hair, no fur, no raiment to disarrange. No silver-trimmed livery-hat to hang on a peg, like Thomas. No grizzle wig to keep free of lice. No hog'd breeches or cambric shirt-bosom to be worked by Mrs. Roill. No shoes to keep soled and blacked. No buckles to polish or under-garments to fetter the nose.

My shell never slips askew. Pupil never dims. Beak never dulls. Leather never pales. Dew glistens on my legs and head, my under-tile. Yes, the mould sometimes clings to my back as I rise in April. Yes, I carry the dishabille of earth for a time.

## Timothy

Mr. Gilbert White writes to nephew Samuel Barker.

"When a man first rouses himself from a deep sleep, he does not look very wise; but nothing can be more squalid and stupid than our friend, when he first comes crawling out of his hibernacula."

Who watches the curate wake? How wise does he look at bed-break? Who judges him so dispassionately?

Late on summer nights he comes into the garden. To see if the bat still flies. To observe by candle-light what moths and earwigs do in the dark. He appears without false hair. Candle held to one side. Pale natural skull like a half moon under his stubble. He clasps together the waist of a coat thrown over his open shirt. Hiding the animal within. Bare calves beneath, spindles of flesh. He does not look very wise, tossing stones into the hedge to make the sedge-bird sing its night song.

Mr. Gilbert White quotes the poet's lines at my advent every spring. Timotheus he calls me then. Timotheus, he says,

> Has rais'd up his head,
> As awak'd from the dead;
> And amaz'd he stares around.

Amaz'd, yes, I do stare around. Awaked from nearer the dead than Mr. Gilbert White imagines.

Light pours in. Soft mist. Walnut tree as bare as it was

when I began digging. Sky as rude. Wind still chafes, and for several nights I return to my winter's nest. But earthworms already writhe in endless venery. Heat of the loam comes on apace. A growing weather. Everything connected to earth by root or foot feels it coming. Has felt it coming for many weeks. Beeches break bud. Apricot blossoms. Dog's-toothed violets blow.

I am late for the first flush of the season. Honeybee warming itself on a clod. Mr. Gilbert White tunning his strong-beer, new green in the wheat. But spring folds open as I wake, returned from my slow submersion. Winter has fled northward on icy legs, carrying off the dead. Sweet reviving breeze calls all the living away from grief. Soft red evenings, day after day. Crimson sun pulsing at the far end of the Hanger. A swarming heat in the air. Good for the husbandman. Warmth runs far ahead of the light, exhausting all of creation. Pitiless ambition of the expanding season.

Gander leads the sow by the ear away from the sitting goose. Birdsong before first light until well into the night. Voice of the cuckoo in the Hanger. Nightingale in the outlet. Wry-neck in the orchard. Mistle thrush, master of the coppice. Chiffchaff fetches an echo at every note. Ring-dove coos, toying on the wing. Snipe pipes and hums overhead until dark.

Alice Beacher and Mr. Gilbert White stand beside the wicket-gate. She is a tortoise taller than he is. He gives her a paper of Savoy seed and three eggs from Gunnory, the bantam hen who broods in the nest over the saddle-cupboard. Alice puts them in her apron. She hears an April grasshopper in the bushes. An impossibility. Small brittle fizzing. Mr. Gilbert White tells her it is really a tiny bird, a grasshopper-lark. She asks why she has never seen one.

"They are such shy, skulking varlets, such hedge-creepers," says Mr. Gilbert White, "that there is no knowing where to have them."

Alice laughs out loud. Claps heavy red hands over her face. She is trying to be polite. But this is as funny as saying that a cow is really a horse or a woman a man.

She thanks Mr. Gilbert White for the seed and eggs. Walks through Ewell-gate into the hop-gardens and fume of spring. Where unhatched grasshoppers whisper aloud in April, just as they've always done. Where fire-drakes cross the skies when shooting stars fall. A world of country people beyond Mr. Gilbert White's garden. Deep in superstition and knowledge, the two almost inseparable. Set upon their ways as he is set upon his.

Men pole their hops around the village. Beyond the garden-back, down the hollow behind Gracious Street. Women bind hop-vines with rushes and crocus leaves. Rows of poles sough in the wind. Oats and barley vegetate. Hopes of the season rise. Wheat thrives again after its winter-burn and sheep are turned in to it, to eat it down and give it stronger roots. Women will be turned in to it later, to weed.

Humans come and go in the garden from first light till last. Pruning, grubbing, burning, sowing, trenching, thinning, planting-out. Repairing the thatched earth-house. Harrowing out the couch-grass. Raising the melon-house, covered with best writing paper—Edmonds and Harper in the Poultry, thick Oliphant cut. Taking up tulips as they fade. Setting out annuals.

A generosity to the plantings here. Asparagus forest. Onions, radishes. Young celery. Endive, to be tied up in early September. Parsnips. Borecole. Garden beans. White cucumbers under hand-glasses. Prickly-seeded spinach. Artichokes. Cauliflowers in rich ground. Vigorous rank growth of potatoes. Autumn lettuces—Coss and Dutch—to winter under straw. Carrots and cabbages laid out by hundreds in long promenades, as if for my parade ground. Cabbage-shade most welcome in the heat of noon.

Goody Hammond sets down her basket. Sinks to her haunches wheezing. Christ my very heart. May comes to this garden and so does she, and all the summer through. In August she gleans in the wheat-stubbles, stooped over the corn. Honest, ignorant. Staunch as stone. Weeds with a short stick, heel of her hand, trowel of strong fingers. Digs and digs. Never lays herself down. Never covers herself over with mould. Never hides from the season. Browned and chapped and leathered. Hair like straw under an ancient livery-hat. Her relief to be on hands and knees again.

## Timothy

Shadows thicken under shrubs, under hazels and walnut. Thunderhead of oak leaves out in the Great Mead. Grass rushes upward. I sink in an edible green sea. Shun the heat. Withdraw beneath my personal cornice. Conceal myself under an awning of dead grass, a garden-mat.

My antic blood. Wicket-gate stands ajar.

．．．．．～

**W**as it an escape? I was eighty-one years old at the time. Age and torpidity are against me. So humans think, who grow torpid in age.

A better question. How do I escape from that nimble-tongued, fleet-footed race? It helps if they leave the wicket-gate open.

The true secret? Walk through the holes in their attention. Easier at my speed than at any faster rate. At evening, larkers stalk the wheat fields, nets spread. Bits of mirror flash behind them. Larks fly into the glittering—and the nets. Larkers cage them. Off they go to wealthy tables, waiting mouths, in Tunbridge and Brighthelmstone.

So it is with humans. Quickness draws their eye. Entangles their attention. What they notice they call reality. But reality is a fence with many holes, a net with many tears. I walk through them slowly. My slowness is deceptively fast.

The humans talk to me. Talk and talk! They say what they

think I'll understand. Hail me from a distance as though I were an unexcitable dog. Child in ill-health. Fellow rake. Sagest of counselors. Ask my thoughts about the barley, the wheat, the hops. About the weather down here. Forget themselves and keep talking. Remember themselves, pretend not to be talking.

I keep my words hidden in the prow of my skull. Mrs. John White crops vegetables for the kitchen. Cuts flowers for the table. Apologizes if she comes upon me meditating in the foliage. Stoops beside me. Lays a warm hand on my shell, admires my mosaic visage, my obsidian eye. A gentle touch.

If I look up at her and say, "Now, then"—what comes next?

Mr. Ralph Churton visits this house at Christmas. Rector of Middleton Cheney. Here the summer of my second escape. They captured me that time near the upper malthouse. Mr. Ralph Churton writes a letter about it to his host, Mr. Gilbert White, who is visiting his brother near London.

Timothy "looks very well," Mr. Ralph Churton assures him, "and says not a syllable of a late elopement."

He thinks he is being ironic.

Mr. Ralph Churton walks through the garden, book in hand. Swallows hawk the hedges behind him. Rustle of a summer wind across the bright sky. Sheep bells, a calf's bawling caught in the breeze. Rill of birdsong. Mr. Ralph Churton glances down at me.

"Behold, the philosophic Timothy!" he says in passing. Raising an arm in salutation.

Irony again. I am some thoughtful centurion, some scribbling consul.

"Behold, the philosophic Churton!" I might say in return.

But he isn't philosophic enough.

My voice would shatter his human solitude. The happiness of his breed depends upon it. The world is theirs to arrange. So they tell themselves. A word or two from me— "Now, then"—and they have all that arranging to do over again.

Can I trust Mr. Gilbert White with a syllable or two? He keeps his countenance turned toward the wild. Knows the elocution of every season, every hour. Tunes his ear to nature's sounds. On foot or horseback every day, over the parish.

Hears the inward melody of a black-cap. Titlark as it feeds in a nearby pasture. Stops stock-still in a meadow, leaning upon his stick. Notes the songs down. Chamois linings to his breeches pockets. Seven pockets to his jacket. Papers in each of them. Sermons, carefully docketed receipts. Most recent letter from Barrington or Molly White. Scraps with dates and birdsongs.

Goodwoman crosses a pasture-field. Daughter by one hand, brindle cow by the other. They see Mr. Gilbert White on a stout Galloway mare. He rises from the saddle. Stands in his stirrups above the rubbed pigskin seat and peers at a nest in an oak bough. Haymakers watch him dismount in the short grass behind them. He kneels stiffly in black leather breeches, worn almost through where they rub against stirrup leathers. Examines a burrow, probes it with his riding-crop. Goodwoman, haymakers, daughter think nothing of it. Brindle cow finds it curious.

Mr. Gilbert White hands the reins to Thomas in a deluge. Steps across the stable-yard. Dirty boots. Dripping bob-wig. Silk oil-skin hood. Carries a fistful of daffy-down-dilly root, for ague. A*rum dracunculus* from the vicarage garden, a cutting from a plant nearly as old as I am. Halves of a broken plover egg in pocket. Old Roman coin. Book of Common Prayer.

Teasing a conjecture in his mind all afternoon, never noticing the downpour. A way to naturalize canary birds. History of noxious insects. Monographies on earthworms or grasses. Life and conversation of the swift. Perhaps just mulling a passage from Linnaeus or Luke. Or the dog that stands on its hind legs to eat from his apricot tree.

Mr. Gilbert White rears the cucumber. Coddles the melon. Improves the polyanth and hyacinth. Wages endless war to keep peaches and nectarines and apricots whole and unblemished. Mellow wall fruit. Catches hornets with half-glasses of his own strong-beer. Birdlime on the end of a hazel twig. Treacle in a bottle. A bounty for wasps' nests and the capture of queens. Fifty thousand wasps destroyed in a single summer. Plundering invaders. "Felon race," he calls them. "Worthless souls"—a harsh judgment even from one who loves apricots. Feeds the nests to the bantam fowl.

Nothing to be done about the humans who steal his wall fruit in the night. Who break the hand-glasses and overset his mounting block once every dozen years.

Sixpence he offers for stories of the bird of many names. Goatsucker, churn-owl, fern-owl, eve-jar, puckeridge, Caprimulgus. The Selborne boys deliver. What they saw, where and when. Old woman living under the Hanger brings him fern-owl eggs. Neighbors, strangers, carry curiosities to him. Young snipe, three snipe's eggs. Common sea-gull still alive. Barnacle goose shot on a Bramshot pond. Butterflies, land-rail, half-fledged fern-owls. Three-pound trout, fine pike. Hairball from the stomach of a fat ox. Male otter, twenty-one pounds, taken in the rivulet below Priory Longmead. Last of its kind ever found in the parish. Pleased to receive it.

Mr. Gilbert White visits the farmers to see what carcasses they nail to the ends of their barns. The countryman's museum. Two albino rooks, a peregrine falcon. Takes up the corpses in his Norway-doe gloves. Runs his fingers against the grain of the feathers. Death-clasped feet, sunken eye, flightless wings.

Sunday comes and he stands before the village in the stone shade of St. Mary's. The Reverend Gilbert White of Selborne in the County of Southampton, Clerk. Fellow of Oriel College, Oxford. Annual stipend. Curate for an absentee vicar. Clean white surplice. Plain, unaffected voice, learned accent. A gentle tone for climactic words. Easter.

"Let us therefore rejoice," Mr. Gilbert White says, reading from his own handwriting, "& be glad on this day of Christian triumph; for our last & most formidable enemy is now destroyed. All his attempts upon the Captain of our salvation were weak & vain; and all the power of Hell cannot now prevail against them that fight under his standard."

He believes in a Captain of salvation and the power of Hell. Death—the most formidable enemy—he says is now destroyed.

"The lamb who was slain now liveth again," he believes.

And so he says aloud to his parishioners.

Though on this earth, the lamb who is slain is supper. It falls to the knife in the butcher's shambles. A sudden start of blood. Behind lime-trees and lilacs, purple and white. Screen of hollyhocks. Planted by Mr. Gilbert White to hide the sight of our most formidable enemy from his street-facing windows. Wasps and blue titmice lie in wait. So does Sarah Dewey. She has been promised a quarter for Mr. Gilbert White's larder. The flesh hangs in a meat-safe of deal and fine fly-wire. Dangles from a walnut tree in this garden. Endless buzzing overhead in sultry weather, when joints spoil.

"The language of birds is very ancient," Mr. Gilbert White also believes, although he does not say so to his parish, "and, like other ancient modes of speech, very elliptical; little is said, but much is meant and understood."

He translates birdsongs. Finds just the analogy. Selborne owls hoot in *vox humana*. Pitches of F sharp, B flat, and A flat. Goose prefers the trumpet. Marsh titmouse sets up the whetting of a saw. Male fern-owl serenades its mate with the clattering of castanets. Beginning just as the Portsmouth evening gun sounds, away to the briny south.

Coincidences mean much to him. Bees swarm as sheep are sheared. Beetles buzz as partridges call. Swifts cease their midsummer flight just as the fern-owl begins to chatter.

Can I trust Mr. Gilbert White with a syllable? Would something shudder within him?

"Now, then," I might say, as he stoops to admire a hyacinth of his own breeding. A knot of worsted tied to the stick that stands before it.

"Now, then."

Before he shoots the greenfinches tearing the blossoms.

"Now, then."

And what comes next?

He is happier translating a language he doesn't know. Happier believing, despite himself, that the language of the brute creation is no language at all. That true speech is human and the rest inarticulate metaphor. Yelling of cats, braying of asses, grunting and whistling of bucks in autumn. Shrieking of swifts on the wing. The sound, he says, of "the juncture when the business of generation is carrying on." A language that humans speak too, beneath the thatch. Cat-like, ass-like, buck-like, swift-like.

To make his metaphors true would beggar him.

His tortoise speaks to him verily in an ancient, elliptical tongue.

"Now, then."

His Captain in rude health one fine Easter morning. Walking among the graves outside St. Mary's.

"Now, then."

All the world to be rearranged.

⌒ · · · · ·

**H**umans crowd around the village square—the Plestor—at evening. Sycamore blooms. Boys play at taw and peg-top. Girls at the work of mothering. The courting gather, over-watched by St. Mary's and her owls and daws and swifts. Decayed laborers bask in the presence of so much youth. Where the great ash recently stood. Huge stubborn mass turned by art into bushels, half-bushels, pecks, gallons, and seedlaps.

During the day, villagers plague Mr. Jack Burbey in his shop. Buying round frocks and stamp-paper. Buttons, mo-hair, and silk. Paying taxes at his counter. Land, window, horse, and servant. Committing themselves for eventual burial.

# Timothy

They walk the single straggling street that rises and bends from one end of Selborne to the other. Pause at Mr. John Carpenter's new bow window. Meager stock of bentware goods, cooperage, nails, and locks. Gossip within the murk of blood, the echoing cries of the shambles over the way. Consult with John Hale for butcher's meat, malt, straw, and oats. Blacksmith grinds a hoe, points a prong. Small comings and goings of the village.

Three hundred and thirteen humans live along the street. Damp clutch of mammals. Writhings of warm flesh and kinship, interwoven in need. Scarcely one without another. Solitude a disease. Solitaries nearly crazy.

Villagers keep pigs and chickens and cats and dogs and swarms of children. No one so poor as to lack a beast or a child. Three men keep caged bullfinches. One a tame bat. Another a buzzard that eats winged ants. Tame snake. Tame raven. Pugnacious young cuckoo found in a hedge-sparrow's nest. Redbreast that sings only in candle-lit rooms. Mr. Jack Burbey kept a brown owl that loved to wash itself. Until it washed too deep and drowned.

Farmers Berriman and Turner raise prize cattle. Dorsetshire ewes that lamb before the year has fairly begun. They treat their kine like daughters newly betrothed to rich young men. Lord Stawel's hunters exercise in a nearby meadow and on the sands around Wolmer-pond. Grooms handle them punctiliously. The grace of courtiers.

Farmer Hale trains a chestnut and a bay in the church-close. Wears a blue smock-frock and knee-high boots. Carries a limber stock-whip. Stops from time to time to rest himself. The horses nibble one another's necks, as if turned out into the after-grass in the shadow of the Hanger.

Forsaken martin-nests along the street. Foul and full of vermin. Mr. Gilbert White knocks them down with a stout stick. It pleases him to watch the birds rebuild. Village cats watch too. They take swifts stooping under the eaves. Young bats emerging from the chimney leads.

The two great motives of love and hunger yaw back and forth through Selborne, driving human and beast alike. To Farmer Parsons and Daniel Loe, the miller, to Mrs. Roill and Martha Knight, nature is worn and familiar. Like the needle-hardened fingers a poor young girl, a Phoebe Cobb, takes as her dowry.

But nature is also a theater of the passions. Fox runs up the midday street. Wrens whistle at it. Humans and dogs rush after in a pack, yowling in equal measure. No telling them apart until the very end. One of the men lifts the creature by the nape. Blood already drying in the fur, on the muzzle. Boys slip leads on the dogs. Is nature the beast or the chase or the drying blood?

Old hunting mare clatters down from the common an into the village street, kicking in pain at her underside. Implores the help of humans, who have none to give her. After a life among them, she dies among them in the night. Her one last question unanswered.

## Timothy

Humans in the parish have little enough command over their own lives. Little enough self-purpose, for all their pother. No one notices the self-command of parish animals except Mr. Gilbert White. He glimpses an inner coherence, a sufficiency. But then he believes in his own coherence, too.

He defers to the evidence of early risers. Country people abroad well before dark. They know where the frost settles. He examines their testimony carefully. Defers to the clemency of his Captain, whose testimony he takes on faith. The wisdom of his god. The wisdom of his god manifested in the works of the creation. As if the works and the creation were somehow separate.

Man of custom and faith. Grandfather's village, grandfather's church, grandfather's Captain. Bible once belonging to his mother. Bound in the skin of her favorite dog. Every few years, he walks the parish bounds as has always been done. A few select villagers, vicar or curate. Three days of tracing the old landmarks. Psalms, cake, cheese, and beer. Thirty miles' perambulating the auspices, the limits of parish responsibility.

Inside the line is Selborne. Everywhere else—outside that line—is elsewhere. Along the little piked close. Down the greenway. Near the stile of the footpath that goes to Noar Hill. Past Priory Ditch, Rushy Lease, and Weavers Down. Dedmans Thorn and Missingham's Mead. Make a shout and an X. Read a gospel. Time out of mind.

· · · · · ⌣

Farmer Spencer finishes his wheat-harvest. Birds gather over the village like thoughts of fall. Taking alarm. Swarming above St. Mary's. Settling and preening for the long flight to come. Raising wings to take in the sun. A crackle of voices. They excite Mr. Gilbert White's most extravagant emotion.

"Such sights as these fill me with enthusiasm!" he says.

Is it departure that moves him? Gathering purpose among the birds? Visible unison as the flock forms? "Consulting," as he says, "when and where they are to go." Is it the swallow's innate sense of the wintering-ground?

Or does the curate imagine the flying? Taking wing over the parish. Striking out under the clouds. House and gardens from a higher vantage than the tower of St. Mary's or the Hanger. And then the downs. Sea beyond. Sunlight scattering on the waves below.

Or is it the change that comes over Selborne when the martins vanish? A sense of being left behind? Only the fernowl, the redwing, and the rain-measurer to divert him. The thought of another winter just ahead. He weighs the improbability of such a flight against the temptation of those warmer climes.

Mr. Gilbert White and his party ride out on Michaelmasday. Thin, bare trail across the open heath. Crowds of swallows roosting on shrubs and bushes. Waiting for fog to clear into a delicate day, warm and bright. They flush with the passage of the horses, who start nervously at the uprising. Sudden applause of so many wings. Not a summer flush— skimming after insects. All on the wing at once, direct. Southward toward the sea, no more to be seen.

Mr. Gilbert White suspects that some of the summer birds winter as I do. Hole in the ground, cavity in a river-bank. "Hiding," he calls it. Cannot persuade himself of the great flights into Africa. Wheatears resting on ships' rigging far out at sea. Flocks in the shrouds. He cannot credit the thought of Selborne's hirundines chattering out of English earshot. No longer *swallow, swift,* or *martin.*

But then his own migrations have been few. To the fens of the Island of Ely when young. To his college at Oxford and back once or twice a year. To Mr. John Mulso at Meonstoke. To Mrs. Rebecca Snooke at Ringmer. To his brothers in London and South Lambeth and Fyfield.

Mrs. John White has been farther abroad. With the Gibraltar garrison. Latitude 36. Chaplain's wife. Capable hands. Complexion hardened by the Spanish sun. Organizing mind. Most unmilitary husband. Too melancholy almost for a cleric. Collector of natural fact and incident. Cadiz by ship. Thirty-seven days back to England, well before the siege commences. Friends and fellow Englishmen catacombed in that rock for months on end. Spanish cannonades after dark. Visible in their faces for years and years after. Badly unstrung by it all.

Mrs. John White hears the birds passing overhead.

Scouting and hurrying low over the water. Seeking the nar-
rowest passage. Southwest over the bay to Tangier. Voices
of home, as English as the prose in her husband's burial
service. "With whom do live the spirits of them." Swallows
carrying Hampshire into Spanish skies. Feathers bleached
by summer. Piss-burnt, the country people say. Color of "an
old weather-beaten brown wig."

Husband dead these dozen years now. Manuscript set
aside, natural history of Gibraltar abandoned. "Not yet published," as his brother kindly puts it. Mr. John White's
legacy? Plaque in a church in Blackburn, Lancashire. Some
cargoes of preserved corpses from Andalusia. A few piles of
paper. Reputation as "a nice observer," "a very exact observer," "a most accurate observer of nature." Also a son—
Gibraltar Jack—and a widow. Long-esteemed by Mr. Gilbert
White. Active disposition, Mrs. John White, ready to put a
helping hand to any household task. Knows the role of the
parish wife. One of the parish widows now.

Arrives my first winter here. Ensconced by spring. Keys in
pocket. Basket in hand. Seeing to provisions. Assisted in
the family by Sarah Dewey. Prepares raspberry and straw-
berry jam, red currant jelly. Preserves cherries and pears
and apples. Wields, with the cook, all those cabbages and
cucumbers. One hundred and ninety-one cut on the 23rd
day of August in the human year 1787. Wealth of the garden.
Curse of the garden.

Mrs. John White wars with insects in Mr. Gilbert White's

wifeless abode. Battle of the Blattae and the house-crickets. She frees the curate for study, field, and church. For parishioners and the creatures of the parish. Vanishes into the intimacy of his esteem. The house unites them. The kin. The naturalist's concerns.

Do the hirundines hide or migrate when winter comes? An urgency to the question that Mr. Gilbert White cannot explain, even to himself.

Second brood of martins just on the wing. Mid-October. Clinging to the street-walls near their nests. Stable and brew-house. Top of the maypole. In these young no idea what to do next. Though the thought is forming.

Mr. Gilbert White asks, "Will these house-martins, some of which were nestlings 12 days ago, shift their quarters at this late season of the Year to the other side of the northern tropic!"

He thinks it improbable. Why go a freakish voyage when a nearby ruin or sandbank beckons? They must lie in secret dormitories the winter through. Beneath the underwood beech at the end of the Hanger.

"It would appear," he writes to persuade himself, "that they never depart three hundred yards from the village."

Evidence is lacking. Probability explains nothing. He has yet to find the winter retreat of the Selborne flocks. Yet to find a torpid martin hidden in a stream-bank. Wild fowls in the forest migrate. Field-fares vanish at summer's end. Ants migrate from their ant-hills—"to the great emolument of the Hirundines." But whether the hirundines themselves depart and to what regions? This he ponders ceaselessly.

To examine the matter of hibernation, I am all the bird he has. Slow domed one at his feet. Tortoise of passage. From the head of the garden to its foot I go. And back. From the fruit-wall to the walnut tree. Sometimes all the way to the wicket-gate and beyond. None of the contagious flurry of swallows and martins. None of the preening and chatter. Nothing to prepare but my nest. No one to convene but myself.

"Timothy the tortoise," Mr. Gilbert White notes, "feeling the approach of cold weather, resorts to the spot where he usually hides, & sleeps in the sun under the warm hedge, tilting his shell on edge that it may take in every ray."

He watches me for clues. As intently as if I were a cucumber swelling in its frame. Has no idea what skies the summer birds traipse when they leave Selborne. Goree? Senegal? Cilician coast? No idea how far and deep I really go where I lie cached in the dead months. No idea where I come from. No notion how dislodged I am.

Martins at play over the fields, ebullient on the wing, thronging. Swallows clustering on the chimneys and cottage-thatch. Awaiting their departure. Then one morning, gone. Village nearly silent. Rooftops unpeopled. Empty, the regions of air above Selborne and the tower of St. Mary's.

But when I rise, birdsong rings in the bowl of Selborne, resounding from Hanger to Lythe and back again. Summer birds already in place. All but the swift, the fern-owl, and the cherry-sucker. Building against the brew-house, high up among the shingles of the church. Gathering moss and thatch from the roofs of houses. Mud from the streets. Reclaiming the nests of the previous year. New-lining them with willow-cotton. Extravagant in song.

"This place," Mr. Gilbert White writes, "is another Anathoth, a place of responses or echoes."

"Answer her, O Anathoth!" is the verse that occurs to him, whenever the echo stirs. Timotheus in Anathoth. The one silent creature.

•  •  •  •  ◡

I met Mr. Gilbert White when he was twenty years old. The human year 1740, and I just come to England. Stolen from the ruins I was basking on. Jut of wall that had stood forever in sight of the Mediterranean Sea. In earshot of its mild tides. Thrust into a heavy bag by hand unseen. Laid in the bottom of a caique, I suppose from the wet that began to pool around me, to sap the cloth. Sounds indistinguishable, human muttering, sharply silenced with a rasping bark. Slap of waves against wood, creak of pitch-seam and oarlock. Audible bulk of a much larger vessel suddenly looming nearby.

Heaved, swung upward, and dropped. Shot out of the bag among naked human feet and into a tangle of netting.

Stowed in darkness. Forgotten. Cavern of tired, labyrinthine odors. Each unclean in its own way. Confused stench. As if the ship had been poulticed with dead fish. Tar and salt and the reek of humans.

We lay by for how long. Then the wind set up a groaning in the ship's bowel where I lay. Keel rising and falling. Swooping, catenary plunge. Months perhaps, many days and weeks certainly. Falling and falling, tumbling away from my terra-cotta city. Its crumbling, overgrown walls. Mosaic floors. Plummeting toward somewhere unsurmisable.

Toward England, as it happened. To what purpose I still cannot guess. Iota in some larger commerce. I withdrew into my shell at the first rough touch on land. Then farther into myself after a time. Embarked impromptu into dormancy. Out of season, out of place, out of country. Stowed away inside myself.

Heir to solitude, like all my kind. Never thought it solitude till I saw the great herds of English gathered thick as gnats about Chichester dock. Rigging against the sky. Quantities of sheep on the wet hills.

Mr. Henry Snooke was the vicar of Ringmer. A churchman, like his nephew, Mr. Gilbert White. But a vicar of the orotund sort. Business in the diocese of Chichester—a ballot—took Mr. Henry Snooke down to that sea-town one day. Chance encounter with a drunken sailor. Disconsolate tortoise wrapped in a scrap of soiled huckaback.

Half a crown swapped hands. One pair rope-chafed, salt-bitten. The other as smooth and white as Mr. Gilbert White's writing paper. I was laid in a covered basket and slung at a servant's side. Free at last from keel-heaving, I think. Only to suffer a swift, brutal trot. Jouncing against the servant's hip for forty miles.

Arrived at a clot of houses on the shoulder of the downs, almost within scent of the sea. Humans all about, a fearsome many. Dark, wet pillars of cloth, nodding as we passed. Wet eye. Pale hand. Bared head. Quizzical bows. Unintelligible sounds flung from their mouths. More humans in one glance than I had seen in a lifetime.

Wet, foreign light of a cold, manicured country. Every direction showed the human in the landscape. Fields stitched together by hedges. Lanes overlooked by rows of yew and elm and lime. District of gates and stiles and paths. Country tended as closely as its sheep, fat as its flocks.

Rooks in the oaks overhead. Treetops tangling, lofty elms. Cross-bills in the Scotch-pine boughs. I was set down between high brick walls in a damp court before the house. Exuding its own fogs. Stationary ship's hold under a column of sky. There to spend forty years. As *Timothy*! As *Tortoise*! Name bestowed by Mr. Henry Snooke. Exclamation by Mrs. Rebecca Snooke, his wife. I had time to discover just who and what she meant.

Forty years. Lifetime of a human born and bred in Selborne. If given an equal chance. Substantial swath of time even to me.

**R**ains failed that first year. Mists on the ponds, where neighbors came for water. Brick-loam in the courtyard and clay beneath. Like living in a china basin. Vast chops and cracks in the soil. In wet years, mud. Blind house-windows staring down. Sometimes catching a flight of sea-driven clouds or a lone gull in a mackerel sky. Tiny, miserable kingdom of one.

I lived under a tuft of hepaticas. To hibernate was merely to daub myself in mire. Whole winters bare-backed, no soil stiff enough to cover me. Wrenched out of the proper seasons. Preposterous rain. Murderous frosts. Weather gone utterly awry. Blood with it. When to dig and when to rise. When to forget.

Great events of those years? Drought that undermined buildings and walls. Black spring of barren cows, whole dairies out of calf. Death by lightning of a coach-horse at grass. Dog-plague that killed them moping. Cannon of the King's review at Portsmouth—firings at Spithead—thundering about the house. Shaking the very earth.

And the demise of Mr. Henry Snooke. Twenty-three years of ignoring me after a chance purchase. A few obvious witticisms among friends. I was perhaps not discursive enough for his tastes. Nor was he likely to talk unbidden to a reptile, unless a company had gathered about him.

Round and round that courtyard I went. Round and

round. Round and round under my chute of sky. Beginning to believe in such a thing as O*ut*. Forty years.

I was intrepid at birth. Hatched in the Cilician brush. Above the warm salt sea. Possessed of the memories I know to be ancient instinct. Broken shells and a common nest the only sign of kin. Mother a scent in the gravel. Father a scent on mother.

Pinnacles of rubble rising out of the slope below me. Human ruins. A devastated city. Dwellings unroofed. Tombs fractured. Cisterns empty. Profound shade under the stone arches, still intact. I came and went and came again. To hear the sea-wind trapped by the walls. To sun myself on so much blank stone. Raucous drift of gulls overhead.

A few furtive goatherds. Burdened ass. Fisherman come ashore to mend his nets. Wait out the African wind or fill his goatskin at the well below the ruins. Wary of the ones who built those walls, buried upslope. Barely willing to set stone upon stone or settle for more than a single night, a single fire.

Who would build such a city only to abandon it? Rubble-masons gone. Kilns cold. Coin-makers forgotten. Lineage broken. Inhabitants vanished. Florid bathers stepping like naked graces from the bath. Water slipping follicle by follicle down the skin. All now desiccated. Baths, aqueducts dry.

Every tale, every memory belonging to that race now lapsed. Some of what they forgot, I remember.

Loggerheads on the sands. Moon on their backs. Dragging a great bulk forward. Sorrow in every landward step. Digging as though distrusting the instinct. Turning to lay as though regretting the ancestry that brings them ashore.

One dam makes for the water. Eye as great as a new mid-winter moon. Sweep of forelegs curved like the blade of a haymaker's scythe. A glimpse of her hovering in the shallows at dawn. Yolk in the sea's white. Relieved of her burden. Freed from the landside tyranny of right side up.

Counterpoise of the deep. Sliding, mid-column, through the pressure of water. To rest on the drift. To slumber so lightly moored to the bottom. To remember to breathe, now and then. To forget the step, step, step, step, step of life on land—that stoic progress—all but once or twice a year.

Were the humans who lived in that place stolen by pirates? Herded off by captors? Borne away by one plague or another? Snatched from their sleep unknowing, as I was?

Or was this grandeur not grand enough? Mr. Gilbert White's question all over again. Hiding or migration? Probability explains nothing. Longevity itself is not long enough to know.

· · · · · ⌣

Every day Mrs. Rebecca Snooke appears. First English-woman, first human, of my close acquaintance. Curious in tortoises. Just past the middle of her long years. Towering overhead. Colossal solitary bloom of cloth. Astonishing headgear, especially on sunny days. Fully rigged with feminine sail overall, though seeming to lack ballast. Rustling and roaring as she walks. Impossible at first to tell just how she is propelled. Launched each morning, with the maid's assistance, after a night in dry-dock.

Pale protected flesh of hands. Childless woman, imperious yet feeling. Still so some forty years later. Gouty. Dropsical in the leg. Palsied for a time. One side shuttered, drooping speech. But a swift recovery. Out almost daily in a carriage until the last. Whirl away in the horse's dust. Scattering good deeds. Improving pamphlets. Mushroom sauce of her own making. Advice and admonishment, strong words of approval and disapproval. Kindly meant. Kindly taken.

"Good morning, Timothy!" for forty years.

"Good evening, Timothy!"

Good evening, Mrs. Snooke!

Dew-damp hem of her garden dress. Pattened feet until her legs grew too swollen. Her particular person-musk, and an aroma, most days, as though she had been hiding herself in the cutting-garden. Taint of cook's citrus-oil on the fingers she extends to me. Trials, in early days, over my palate. Seed-cake, cat's-meat, chicken liver, raw egg, calf's-foot jelly. Unspeakable delicacies carried from her plate to the border where I lie.

"Timothy!" she cries. "Try some!"

At last the delicacies ended or I would have wasted away to a cavity. Lettuce, kidney beans, a wafer of cucumber. Dandelion or sowthistle when in season. Good Ringmer apples, pears, and grapes. Those sufficed. Even delectable in dry autumns. Not a poppy leaf to be had for forty years. Grateful for an arbitrary stomach, able to fast almost at will.

Forty years Mrs. Rebecca Snooke teeters around her courtyard. Increasingly vertiginous. Cup and saucer in one hand on fair days. Work-basket sometimes dangling from an elbow. Volume of religious poems in her fingers. Feet peeping out from under her skirts like goslings under a spring goose. Thinks nothing of walking and talking at the same time. Walking and talking while thinking of something else entirely. Took up the stick for a while, but that was just another limb in the way.

Mr. Gilbert White appears once or twice in autumn and spring. Slender, knobby, compared to the plush vicar of Ringmer. Dry, deliberate manner in the pulpit. Learned decorum in his correspondence with men of science. But a warmth, a somehow precise playfulness in the family. Hive of questions, always buzzing. Monster of interrogation. Always felt his eye fixed upon me. Curiosity amok.

Still a young man at first. Frugality not quite confirmed in his character. Yet already a careful keeper of accounts. A settled habit. Receipts docketed. Balance carried forward. Able to stretch £20 as far as Mr. John Mulso's £40. Shilling lost at cards in the common room. Sixpence to read the third and fourth volumes of *Amelia*. Considerably more for a party at the Three Goats. To purchase Fairey Queen, a liver-colored spaniel-bitch of the Blenheim-breed. A man of sport.

Yet also two hundred broccoli plants. Three hundred Savoys. Two silver and one Scotch fir. Fifteen loads of melon-earth from Dorton. The new edition of Miller. Hitt's book on wall fruit. Mr. John Ray's *Methodus*.

Kin by close blood, Mrs. Rebecca Snooke. Mr. Gilbert White's father's sister. (So precise they are in the degrees of kinship!) And yet how these humans differ in appearance, compared to the resemblance of tortoises one to another, kin or no kin. Mr. Gilbert White was always struck by the fact that I recognized Mrs. Rebecca Snooke.

She comes into the courtyard waving a lettuce-leaf.

Calling from on high, "*Timothy! Timothy!*"

Who else could it have been? In forty years only a few humans ever entered that courtyard. Gardeners, maids, young Whites, select friends, Mr. Manning, the doctor. Each one as different as a rook from a redbreast.

Was Mr. Gilbert White never struck by the fact that Mrs. Rebecca Snooke recognized me? If another of my kind had walked up to her on that pebbled path, could she have told the difference? Or would that tortoise have been *Timothy* too? She knew little enough about me in the end.

"I was much taken," Mr. Gilbert White wrote of me, "with

its sagacity in discerning those that do it kind offices: for, as soon as the good old lady comes in sight who has waited on it for more than thirty years, it hobbles towards its benefactress with awkward alacrity; but remains inattentive to strangers. Thus not only '*the ox knoweth his owner, and the ass his master's crib,*' but the most abject reptile and torpid of beings distinguishes the hand that feeds it, and is touched with the feelings of gratitude!"

Good old lady she was. Yet consider the levity, the dry prolixity of Mr. Gilbert White's words. The casual human irony when talking about animals. "Awkward alacrity"— "most abject reptile and torpid of beings"—this I expect. "Ox" and "ass" I pass by, as I do "owner" and "master." Such words come naturally to humans. Students of property as well as kinship. Kinship a property in each other.

But place Mrs. Rebecca Snooke in a brick box apart from her natural kind. Where she cannot eat her natural food or dig her natural bed. Let her be fed twice a day, albeit cheerfully, by one who keeps her there. Be kind and withhold the drowning rains, the killing frosts. Year after year for forty years. Would she say she has been waited on? Or would another word occur to her?

Mrs. Rebecca Snooke preserved the empty shells of other tortoises. On a lacquered table inside the house, in a room over the hall. Small and hinged, like double-lidded snuffboxes. She dressed her hair with hawksbill combs. A pair of box turtles roamed some distant province of the garden, well beyond my walls. Once upon some other time. Were they rumor only?

To her nephew, in those days, I am chiefly "Mrs. Snooke's present *living* tortoise." The emphasis is his, and mine. Thus the history of tortoise-husbandry among the Snookes.

. . . . . ⌣

I was the leaseholder of my own existence in Ringmer. Awaiting the final freehold of death. But it was she who died, late one winter. Early March. Earthed in still I lay. Aged nearly eighty-six she was, ancient for a human. Merely respectable for a tortoise.

Sexton buried her beside the body of Mr. Henry Snooke in Ringmer church. St. Mary the Virgin. A few grim words, full of the hope but not the rejoicing of spiritual continuance. Common grave a hybernaculum till their desired arising in some later, better world. How long they will wait for that spring no one at the grave-side can say.

Forty years I watched Mrs. Rebecca Snooke capsizing. Profusion of days killed her in the end. She died an ancient in her village. Revered as much for being old as for being neighborly, charitable, dutiful. She taught me how it is to be human. Kind, unkind, agile, halt, forgetful, almost sick with memory. Corrupted and hectored by time.

What afflicts these beings more than their longevity, their pride—their *altitude*—is the sad dissolving of the pith itself. Badly fitted for the age they attain. Blood pooled when she sat. Bones disconnected. Skin turned to crape. She became more and more an affair of cloth and stiffeners. A lady's-maid's construction. Native vigor sapped. Harder and harder to bend down. Harder and harder to stand up. Little to eat and still less sleep.

Could she see that I was not keeping pace with her? That she was aging on her own, without me? I receded from her. She from me. And so she never knew that in forty years of her own aging I had barely aged a day. The secret of our longevity, the tortoises. Young till the very end.

It was a well-intended slavery, living at Ringmer. Apprenticed for life in the role of curio. Forever bounded by four brick walls. Fed by human hands.

I was fashionable, you see. We were fashionable, the tortoises, a fashion only just beginning. Not in Ringmer or Selborne alone. Tortoises all across the ecclesiastical countryside, none of us native. Find a clerical establishment of a certain outlook and behold! Tortoise in the garden. Vicars and curates examine their reptiles the way they examine the *Clergyman's Intelligencer* or Ecton's guide to parish incomes. Consult us, round Easter, like clocks. Who rises?

A tortoise a century old returns to life in a neighboring village. The report goes out. Mr. Loveday's tortoise at Caversham surfaces. Mr. Loveday writes to say so, until the day the old man is gathered-in like a ripe stock of corn. Out goes the news when I surface in Ringmer. The vicars humiliate themselves with us. A tortoise lives even longer than a bishop.

Yet they cannot quiet their human-ness. Humility never comes naturally to their meditations. Pride of the vertical. Assurance of those who wear hair, even if not their own. Pomp of warm-bloodedness. An equilibrium they mistake for rationality. Over-certainty about their station in life.

In the book that made his name, and mine, Mr. Gilbert White writes these words: "It is a matter of wonder to find that Providence should bestow such a profusion of days, such a seeming waste of longevity, on a reptile that appears to relish it so little as to squander more than two thirds of its existence in a joyless stupor, and be lost to all sensation for months together in the profoundest of slumbers."

A clerical toast! Providence and a profusion of days!

Mr. Gilbert White's nightly stupors. How joyful are they? Is he lost to sensation in his own profound slumbers? Or does he sometimes dream, as I do, more vividly than waking itself? Where is the particular profit in his personal longevity?

Mr. Gilbert White values the open eye more than the shut. Common mistake. The sensation I lose in hibernating is the one of separation. Of having been plucked from my ancestry so many years ago. Mr. Gilbert White would be surprised to learn how deeply I relish my longevity. How infinitely it has been extended since I was stolen from myself.

Clerics number their days by numbering ours. Question their god. As if we were skulls tumbled out of a swollen graveyard. Dug up from under the church-paving. No being apportions its life span. To them a tortoise seems to squander existence. Dozing too often, no work at hand, living on and on and on. If so, then their god must have squandered existence too.

The worst of the clerics look upon us as a meal gone missing. Walking tureen of turtle soup. Glare at their congregation in the same hungry way.

The best of them see in us an inherent mystery. Perhaps that is why Mr. Gilbert White watches so closely. The real question he knows. Why any creature is allotted time on this earth. No matter how brief or how long. He knows this. Even if he hides the question from himself.

〜 • • • • •

Burying done. Mr. Gilbert White, nearly sixty years old, pries me out of my winter's depression in Mrs. Rebecca Snooke's brick courtyard. Not the picture of resurrection he preaches from the pulpit. Captain of salvation with a trowel in his hand. Parson's black coat and mud-stained shoes. Probing in a shallow graveyard for a soul to raise. I hiss at him for his disrespect, his unseasonableness.

He places me in a wooden box filled with earth and moss. Ship-board again for me, I think. Sea-borne back to the Cilician coast, to my antique city. Great wrong set right at last.

But no. Eighty miles in post-chaises. Dismal hostelry. Rocking and pitching across the south of England. Through the child-rhyme villages of Uckfield, Cuckfield, Horseham, and Dorking. My only contentment Mr. Gilbert White's retching from the violence of the vehicle's motion.

I know now he intended an act of kindness. Also a chance to watch me more closely. My imperfect Ringmer dormitory, meager winter clay on my back, wilted shade—these he had witnessed. He ignored my hissing, as I ignored his rheumy coughing. Did his best to cushion me from the concussions of travel by post-chaise, from which he suffered far more than I did.

And so on not to the sea but to another clot of houses. Another fearsome lot of humans, though less forbidding after forty years among them. To this place, to Selborne. A town not high on the chalk downs, like Ringmer, but lodged in a crevice between the hills. Under the beeches and oaks. Sheltered vale beneath the winds.

Arrived at last. Surrendered into a garden beneath the brow of the Hanger. Just as spring begins. Forty years after first being carried into this damp woolen country. Suddenly a sweet, green season. A hint, even in March, of what is to come. Peaches and nectarines bloom on the only wall in sight. Grapes thrive on the house itself. Living borders of shrubs and flowers instead of the mute red walls of my former courtyard. Laurel, laburnum, and jonquil, crowded with birds all summer long. Cascades of scent, blossom, and pollen. Almost overpowering when sun lifts the dew from the garden.

Frogs croak as I come fully awake. Studding ponds with their spawn. Nuthatch clatters in the woods, and the storm-cock sings. Early swallows flitter. Bees above the cucumber frames, waiting for Mr. Gilbert White to open the lights. Blossoms inside daubed with honey to encourage the setting of fruit.

Willows flower in the coppices. Mistle thrush nests in the garden-traffic to save her brood from magpies. Hedgehogs mine the grass-walks for plantain roots. Puff-balls and fairy-rings surface. The wood-lark sings in air all night long. Atmosphere already crowded with insects. Rising and falling in the sunlight streaming down the Hanger. Gossamer.

A man called Thomas appears that first day. Mr. Gilbert White asks him to dig a hole for me. As unexpected as if I had been asked to dig a grave for Mrs. Rebecca Snooke. Places me in it himself.

I dig out and march twice over the precincts of the garden. Almost gratified, in my journey-jumbled, winter-dreary state. The extent of my new demesne. The confines seem more than ample. Smooth avenues of sand and grass and brick. Long brick-walk from the kitchen to the wicket-gate. Glimpse of the board-statue of Hesperian Hercules in the distance. Pausing from his labors, ever patient, in the Great Mead. Concourse of turf thick beneath my claws. Now, to do something about the weather.

## Timothy

Here I roam at large. Stand at the edge of the ha-ha and survey this spacious world. If rain disturbs my reflections, I withdraw to the rhubarb or the lee of the cucumber frame. Salad myself on the grass-walks. Devour what lettuces I choose, even to the detriment of Mr. Gilbert White's table. Sojourn among the melons and the cardoon trunks. The cabbage-cordons. Meditate in the onions. The carrot ranks. The asparagus forest. Muse near the hedge against Benham's yard, where chickens wait for the wheat-sheaf wagons to pass. I lie abroad among hyacinths. Pause to feed upon a globe-thistle. Bathe in the liquid scent of peonies. Feast on the leaves of poppies. Poppies!

That first Selborne autumn, I sleep under a Marvel of Peru. In the warm shelter of the fruit wall, disbelieving. Glow-worms twinkle in the lanes. I drowse my way toward another rude English winter. Hen-coop over my back to keep the dogs from nosing too closely. Mr. Gilbert White affords me a good armful of straw. Is he this kind to all his parishioners? Benevolence on his part. And if awkward, that is because one creature's courtesies are so often another's insults.

$\bullet \quad \bullet \quad \bullet \quad \bullet \quad \sim$

It took me many months among them to trust that humans could keep from falling over. Their paces, forward and backward, still seem little more than falling forestalled one foot at a time. Side-to-side shuffling of a raven. Not nearly as solid on their feet as a hen scratching after crumbs in the street.

Tottering, two-legged, stilt-gaited beasts. Only at a distance can I see them whole. Against the quincunx on Baker's Hill. Cutting the sainfoin. Tacking vines along the fruit wall when I am resting in the laurel hedge. Up close, they steeple over me, eclipsing the sun. Pale pompion heads lurching across the sky. As if the beeches had walked down from the Hanger to lour over the haymakers.

For a time I flinched whenever a human approached. Especially Mr. Henry Snooke, who carried such a stoup of belly before him. The feet would stop but the top might timber onto me. I still doubt the stability of the species. All that brain-bulk merely to prop them up? Or are they less top-heavy than they appear?

Thunderstorm visits Selborne. Vast floods! Hail near two feet deep! Bottle-blue wind uproots beech trees on the Hanger. Shrieks down the street. Tearing thatch and tiles from the roofs of the village. Battering windows. Toppling chimney pots and felling old wooden Hercules in the Great Mead. Scarcely levels a single human.

Still, to see Goody Hammond on hands and knees weeding among the lettuces—the relief is not hers alone.

How these humans dispose themselves! Unlike anything else in creation. Or rather like everything else in creation all at once. Legs of one beast. Arms of another. Proportions all awry to a tortoise's eye. Torso too squat. Too little neck. Vastly too much leg. Hands like creatures unto themselves. Senses delicately balanced. And yet each sense dulled by mental acuity. Reason in place of a good nose. Logic instead of a tail. Faith instead of the certain knowledge of instinct. Superstition instead of a shell.

Postures stiffen as age and religion set in. Yet even the ancient ones fling their limbs in all directions. Restless as a pullet with mites. As if, by rising into an upright gait, humans had forgotten how to set their extremities at ease.

A couple rushes from St. Mary's. Farmer Turner, seventy-one, and his housekeeper bride, Rose Rawkins, sixty-nine. A jig in their steps despite their age. Mrs. Andrew Etty, the vicar's widow, still rides her mare from Selborne to Alton and back. Tumbling if the horse tumbles, as it sometimes does. Skirts wrung in the dust. Defensive as a hedgehog.

Mr. Thomas Barker—by no means young—starts up from the breakfast table. Runs a race around Baker's Hill against Samuel, his son, not half his age. Timed by Mr. Gilbert White's watch. One minute and a quarter for the straight-bellied old man. Less than a minute for the young one. Mr. Barker rides one hundred and eighteen miles in three days, from Lyndon to Selborne. Walks ahead, wig in hand, while the horses bait themselves at an inn. As though they had hired him to scout the way. A sandy road through dappled shade.

The thatcher, Richard Butler, laying bright new thatch. Clambers over the ridge-poles in the village. Climbs atop mounds of hay in the barnyard, roofing the ricks against winter. Shilling and ninepence. "For theatching of a heavy Reck," he likes to say. Nimble as the titmouse hanging upside down. Two of a kind. Titmouse pulling straws from the eaves with its beak. Undoing the thatcher's work, giving houses a ragged appearance.

A man in a dry year climbs sixty-three feet down Mr. Gilbert White's well. Like a bat in a chimney to gnaw the bacon. Climbs back out when he's done with his cleaning, carrying taws and marbles thrown in long ago. What surprises Mr. Gilbert White isn't the in and out. It's the sight of his old taws and marbles.

Farmer Town, of more than ordinary girth, gets a leg up from the wide-eyed ostler at The Compasses. Rolls onto the saddle like an overfull oat-sack. The horse widens its legs without looking round. Cuts a fine figure on horseback, Farmer Town believes. The real drama is dismounting.

Richard Horley edges a hip and knee under the outstretched hind-leg of Miller. Mr. Gilbert White's ailing portmanteau horse. Miller leans against the blacksmith. Leg goes limp. Sole of the hoof upturned. Miller reaches round to tug at the farrier's apron. A tangle of human and equine limbs.

In the meadow the dairy-maid pitches herself beside a spotted cow's udder. Leans her head against the flank. Two teats for the calf standing opposite. The rest for her. Shearer and sheep move almost as one. Cotillion of wool.

Mr. Ralph Churton absently picks his teeth with the nib

of a pen. Body going about its business while the mind is elsewhere. Probes an ear with a twist of paper. Reaches right around behind himself to un-crevice his breeches. The elegant scratch the one inaccessible spot on their spines with an ivory tool contrived for the purpose or the brass end of a walking stick. The rest rub up against a tree or fence, like a fatting hog in a wattle pen.

Notable woman and her girl in the hop-garden. Twenty-four bushels of hops they pick in a single September day. Always a gambling crop. In good years thirty tons from the hop-grounds of Selborne. In good years, 3 shillings a day, £2,000 to the parish as a whole. All from the dexterous fingers of women and girls. When a tempest destroys the Kentish crop and Canterbury fails, there are cheerful faces in Selborne. In bad years, hop-women complain of the cold. Wetted through and through in the picking.

Gleaners come home from the wheat stubbles. Loaded with bundles. Children burdened no less. Over head and ears in the sheaves. Their weight in grain and straw and spiders.

Young of this village hang by the knees—that puzzling joint—from tree-limbs. I watch in amazement. Also horror. Blood rushes to the head. Roar of the red ocean in their ears. Children roll side-long down the Bostal. Pitch into summer-cocks from fences and barn-eaves. Vault streams on the back of a pole. Ride the oxen in their stalls when the farmers aren't looking. Recline upon horses as though their backs were as broad as the sheep-down itself.

Not a child in Selborne who hasn't been bruised or broken, willingly. Laughing until tears come in earnest. Smelling like loam and stale pond. Like horse, sheep, pig, and the dung of each. Sour wary tang of unwashed human flesh.

And Daniel Wheeler's boy? Ah, Daniel Wheeler's boy is an ape of motion, an imp of impulse. Walks the length of the ha-ha on his hands. Shins up the maypole to touch the fane. Hops down the brick-walk, to the distraction of Rover and Fyfield, who bark as they would at intruders.

Lad to plunder the honey-buzzard's nest in the beech-tops? Worry hoopoes until they desert this parish? Climb down a cavern newly opened under the cart-way? Display an agility either less or more than human? This is the boy that is chosen.

· · · · ⌒

**H**eron's sinuous neck encompasses everything within its reach. Forward and backward, upward and down. Curving and recurving as she hunts in the stream, motionless. Even the human arm is not this lithe. Yet the heron cannot sit on her tail, long leg thrown over the rail of a peat-cart, as I have seen William Marshall do. Cannot quote gospel with a pipe of tobacco thrust into the corner of her mouth.

# Timothy

In spring the small tribe of vipers reappears as I am surfacing. Circling all the way round upon themselves. But they purchase extreme flexibility at the cost of extremities. Becoming a single extremity. Their suppleness is all horizontal.

Viper-dam cannot lean doubled-over against an oak-tree, like a reaper giving out in summer's great heat. Viper-sire cannot halt at arms like a soldier in Burgoyne's light horse. Pausing in his march over the Sussex downs to Portsmouth and America. Cannot spit into the bushes while he makes water standing, like a common hind.

Young vipers already viperous at birth—gaping and menacing. But they cannot kneel on a brick floor with a scrub-brush. Beat up butter and print it, as the girls of this village are taught to do. Cannot whisk the nose-flies that fret the horses as they plow, little baskets tied over the muzzles.

Frogs migrate across the parish in July. Creatures no larger than the nub of my tail. Trooping into the lanes in vast numbers and to the top of the Hanger. Fore-limbs and hind-limbs as different from each other as human arms and legs. How do their fore-limbs serve these amphibians? Perhaps only in what Mr. Gilbert White delicately calls their "amours." Intrigues notorious to every creature in Selborne. Frogs sticking "upon each other's backs for a month together in spring."

Yet the inestimable frog-tongue sings only the same vernal tune every year. Incapable of gossip.

Mr. Gilbert White reads the marriage service soberly.

"In the time of man's innocency . . . mystical union . . . not by any to be enterprised . . . to satisfy men's carnal lusts and appetites, like brute beasts that have no understanding . . ."

Wishes, as he reads, that the bride were as slender-waisted as his hay-rick at the end of a bitter winter. Knowing glances in the congregation. Whispered word among the wives, some of whom came less than virginal to wedlock themselves. No shame at all from the frog's point of view. No cause to vary one's song. Endlessly concupiscent melody of Earth.

～ • • • • •

**A**gility, dexterity, these are not enough for humans. Not enough to be able to see most of one's body at a glance. Necessary also to witness one's very own face. To know it in the glass, the shop-window, the knife-blade, the pond. To wink at oneself. To grin like a horse with lips pulled back. To offer oneself the compliment of a sly, urbane glance. As if one wouldn't know oneself coming down the street. Judging that face, those features as if they belonged to a stranger.

"Not a bad-looking fellow!"

"How this blue satin becomes my complexion!"

A metaphysical dexterity exceeding all the rest of creation.

# Timothy

In what are humans stranger than this? To live in a world peopled by their own reflections. By shadows that rise up, life-like, to claim relation. Not in puzzlement or hostility, like a dog before the strange, scentless beast in the mirror. Not in blank unnoticing, like a water-eft on the edge of its well-bucket. Unable to admire its yellow belly. Take in its black, warty fin and tail.

But to greet oneself knowingly, like Mr. John Mulso. His reflection more intimate, better-loved than even his well-loved family. Demands more easily satisfied. More easily disregarded. Such a welcome surprise when that bold, laughing face turns up. Looking back unexpectedly in a hallway mirror. So comfortably disinclined to exert itself. Engaging wink. Distinguished profile. So easy to dismiss when dinner calls. Only to turn up in the silver. A perfect companion.

How elaborate the mirror's protocol! How decorous! How it resists certain angles! Miss Molly White's only affectation is quoting Latin. Yet she tries to behold her backside while standing beside the parlor window. Judging the effect of a newly turned ribbon. The glass refuses to show the hind side to her. For the rear view humans must take each other's word. They do so with characteristic reluctance.

In all my life, I have never seen either of my hind feet. I surmise their shape from my front feet and from the feel of being in them. From encounters with my own kind long ago. Much less have I seen the ridge-line of my carapace or the mottling of my under-tiles. I only intuit that my tail is there.

And were I to come upon my face as it came upon me, it would look back at me implacably, unvarying. I wear a good round expression suited to all my needs, to every occasion. As do most creatures on this earth. An everyday and Sunday, coronation and burial face. To see it once would be to have seen it for all time.

Not like the molten features these humans wear. They look again and again and never find the same visage twice. Mrs. Henry White stares into her hand-mirror as though it were a fraud upon her intelligence. Always showing her the wrong reflection. A woman older and somehow coarser than she expects to find. Not at all the woman within.

I do not live in a prison of choices, like humans. I have the one gait, faster or slower. Stand on all my feet or rest on my plastron. Extend my limbs and head and tail. Or not. Mobility limited by human standards. Flight limited by avian standards. All the suppleness necessary to a tortoise. Balance perfect.

· · · · · ◡

**W**hat would I do with those human paces and postures? Those abrupt gestures? Useless in a solitary creature. I look at those mobile faces and see a desperate urge for company. I look at that upright posture and see only sore necks and punishing feet.

Mr. Gilbert White ponders my carapace. Supposes that my shell imprisons me. Does the skull imprison the brain? "Coffined" is the word that occurs to more than one of his friends. They will know when they are coffined how inapt that word is. Mr. Gilbert White suspects that my inability to step out of my shell precludes "all activity and disposition for enterprise."

As if what goads these people into labor is their lack of armor. I feel no want or limitation. The living day is enterprise enough.

Humans confuse the matter of shell and tortoise. Container for the thing contained. Talk as though they were two and not one. As though the part of the tortoise that is not shell were as stout as the carapace itself. A structure, Mr. Gilbert White has written of my own, "that would secure it against the wheel of a loaded cart." An experiment he hesitates to try.

Each creature judges the condition of others and finds all but its own imperfect. Rover sleeps on his belly in the grass. One ear pricked for a moment, then topples over, waking him up. A gelding in the after-grass scratches its jaw with a hind hoof. Wish I could do the same when smother-flies shower down or lice prevail or fern-chafers invade the garden. But then a grass-horse cannot carry its stall with it when lying out on rainy nights.

Bantam hens sprawl in the yard after ruffling a cloud of

dust into their feathers. Wings and legs extended. Eyelids sealed like death on a hot summer day. Should the sparrow-hawk stoop, to the terror of village dames, safety lies too far away for the chickens. Unless Will Tanner and his gun are ready. Sparrow-hawk can have none of me.

Sheep of the parish seem the most pampered of beings. Fortunes tied intimately to humans. Carefully washed and shorn in June. Flocks closely tended. Moved as often as possible to graze on fresh grass or green wheat or fields of spoiled barley. Belly-deep in their proper food. Yet when rains fall, sheep die, even on so wholesome a spot as the commons. On low ground they rot, seeming to breed maggots. Ewes die in lambing. Lambs that come in the wrong weather freeze where they fall.

Some winters the flocks tear their fleece trying to get at the lice that tease them. Magpies ride their backs, eating the lice. Sheep are "little aware," Mr. Gilbert White notes, "that their eyes are in no small danger; & that their assiduous friends would be glad of an opportunity of picking their bones." The humans—assiduous friends of sheep—are the ones to pick their bones at last. Mutton and grass-lamb, once butcher Hale has done with the flock.

Even the Selborne rooks. Playful as they are, tumbling on wing in the gaiety of their hearts. Plagued by their own society. Constant fighting. Perpetual destruction of nests. Proceedings, Mr. Gilbert White notes, "inconsistent with living in such close community."

Soot-dark birds, thousands of them. Wheeling through

the air as they gather on their nests in the rook-village on the Hanger at evening. Dusk rings with obstreperous complaint. Un-neighborly contention before they retire to roost in the woods of Tisted or Ropley with the last gleam of light.

Rook-chiding over the common resembles a murmuring. So Mr. Gilbert White fancies. "The cry of a pack of hounds in hollow, echoing woods, or the rushing of the wind in tall trees, or the tumbling of the tide upon a pebbly shore."

The fond illusion of distance. Romantic effect of perspective. Mr. Gilbert White would loathe such clamorous, dissenting neighbors any closer at hand. As bad in their own way as fumes from the charcoal-making in Farmer Spencer's orchard.

And what do the rooks on high make of Mr. Gilbert White and his fellow humans? Is he the subject of their speculations—born of perspective—as they peer down on Selborne? Do they tell a story about the slight, flightless man who lives beyond the ha-ha? Do they admire humans or fear them from that distance? Or do they notice only the rook-splendid chaos of their own domestic squabbles?

· · · · ⌣

**A**bove all, Mr. Gilbert White is a man of system. Naturalist, physico-theologist. He lives in inches and ounces and hours and degrees. Matter flows in upon him. New information crowds in every day. He examines the forest sand through a microscope—smooth from collision, a yellow color. Watches the weather glass closely. Supine is the man who fails to put out his thermometer.

Weather on March 20, 1780, the day I was first set loose in Selborne? Dark, moist, and mild. Fifty degrees. Southwest wind. Full moon. Crocuses in high bloom. A matter of record.

Mr. Gilbert White chronicles rain and snow and barometric pressure. As if they were baptisms and burials and marriages in the parish register—the death of Anne Wheeler, age twenty-four, last year, or the union of William Trimming and Elizabeth Bartholomew. The burial, just a few days ago, of Mary Burbey, age sixteen, of this parish, "by me, Gil. White curate." Sixteen years and gone. A mayfly's life.

The human year 1751, Mr. Gilbert White records, "was one of the wettest Years in the memory of Man." He is able to report that the 24th of August, 1764, was "the fourth most beautiful harvest-day that ever was seen." Glass very high.

"Those that had the most patience will have by much the best corn," he declares, like the parson he is.

He identifies four hundred and thirty-nine local plants. Traveler's joy, twayblade, eye-bright cow-wheat, go-to-bed-at-noon. Knee-holly, or butcher's broom. Knows the common tongue for plants and the learned one too. Which birds possess a local name—the sit-ye-down. And which don't—Regulus non cristatus.

## Timothy

Mr. Gilbert White items the fishes in Gracious Street stream and the Well-head stream. Bull's head or miller's thumb, trout, eel, lampern, and stickleback. Packs them in a little earthen pot full of moss. Bound for London to be engraved. Tracks the margins to discover the water vole, where it swims and dives.

Probes the oat-ricks for the grand rendezvous of harvest mice. Clocks the rate at which the white owl feeds its young. Once every five minutes, beginning at sunset, when mice start to run. He works at sorting the profusion of beetles. Understanding the ants. Midges like smoke as they rise and fall on a warm May morning.

Early black grape climbs the study wall. Mrs. Rebecca Snooke's variety. Thomas stands at the vines all morning, removing an infestation of beetles. A private passion of his own. Killing them one by one. Moving on to the goose-berries.

In the window above, the scent of spices and stale flesh. Damp feathers, acrid air. Mr. Gilbert White works at a table. Eviscerating a long-legged plover, drawing the en-trails. Stuffing its skin with salt, pepper, and alum, ginger, cloves, and camphor. A little down the throat. Some tow in the abdomen for a life-like shape. Divides the weight of the bird by its length of leg. The result, he notes: a ten-foot flamingo.

The study is full of small corpses, labeled, shelved, pre-served. Villagers and country people—humans generally—

are always good for a supply of small corpses. Boys especially. Knock at the door means a dead bird in a male-child's hands. Clutch of mottled eggs in a poor woman's basket. Limp carcass over the shoulder of a yeoman's son. Lord Stawel's servant with a curious pheasant.

Some creatures die in Selborne—sheep and pigs—because that is their purpose. Some—the otter—die merely because they stray into sight. Others are sacrificed—fowl by the hundreds—to the sporting instinct in humans, a passion almost beyond inhibition. Mr. Gilbert White is one of the few to have stilled that instinct in himself.

"When I was a sportsman," he now likes to say of his youth. Pointers in turnip-fields. Stone-curlews rising from the crop. Gunpowder and shot. Sixpence for gun-cleaning. Regular items in Mr. Gilbert White's ledger long ago. Inhospitably fetching down "our visitants, the birds of passage," writes Mr. John Mulso of those far-off days.

Out comes the firearm now to protect the garden. To keep house-sparrows out of the house-martins' nests. Greenfinches from the blossoms. Blackbirds and thrushes from plundering the fruit. And he fires at birds—or causes them to be fired at—to answer his insatiable curiosity. To know what he sees.

Mr. Gilbert White commands the muzzles, the nets and traps, of the entire parish and beyond. Causes a nuthatch to be shot in the act of clattering its beak against wood. To know whence that sound arises. A friend procures a sandpiper for Mr. Gilbert White's collection. Another a butcher-bird. A neighbor downs a house-martin for him in early May. To learn whether martins are lean and emaciated when they appear for the season. Fat and fleshy and dead is how that one is. Stomach full of the legs and wings of beetles.

Thus he ensures the accuracy of his autopsia. Evidence of his own eye. Direct examination only to be trusted. Antidote to the bad habit of "comparing one animal to the other by memory." The fallacy of analogous reasoning. All the naturalist's knowledge, writes one of that kind, comes from "killing animals, and examining them when dead."

Mr. Gilbert White preserves for reference a pair of harvest-mice in brandy. Stores specimens from Gibraltar—packed long ago by Mrs. John White on her husband's behalf. Dried plants and preserved birds. A little cargo of curiosities. Accidental samples of the vine-eating beetles that preoccupy Thomas. Boxes from a Levant ship. Quarantined at Stangate Creek. Loaded on the Southampton Coach to be left at the Swan Inn at Alton.

A large fine *Vespa. Merops apiaster.* Puffin. Razor-bill. Various fishes. A vulture's head and feet. The rest of the carcass eaten by the starving fishermen who found it dead and floating in the sea.

Mr. Gilbert White finds the ring ousel, when dressed for the table, "well-tasted, & juicy, & in high condition for plumpness." Bittern shot in a shrub-wood tastes like teal, though not so delicate. Intestines covered with fat. Bird that goes "crex, crex" in wet meadows and bean-fields—a land-rail—turns out fat and tender. Flavored like the flesh of a woodcock, with a large and delicate liver.

Does Mr. Gilbert White merely keep the bills of animal mortality? Does his system, his curiosity, create a market? But up springs a market for animal flesh wherever there are humans. Female woodcock shot in Selborne, sent to London. Finds a buyer as it is being carried along the street. Porter offered a guinea for it. So succulent is the purchase.

Daniel Wheeler's boy comes into the garden. He sizes me up, thinks avoirdupois and shillings and scarcity. I weigh six pounds thirteen ounces and am extremely rare. Original price half a crown, more than fifty years ago. Undervalued even then.

But Daniel Wheeler's boy has no market for me. I live in the asparagus of his only buyer. I size him up too. Shanks like hop-poles. Malevolent squint. No market for him either. Not if England is at peace.

⌣ • • • • •

System isn't everything. But without system, Mr. Gilbert White notes, "the field of Nature would be a pathless wilderness."

He has never seen a pathless wilderness. Selborne parish is groomed as clean as the brick floor in his kitchen.

Woods, down, heath-forest, mead. Field, common, stream-bottom, pasture. Bog, pond, high-wood, hedge. Coppice, stubbles, hanger. Each shaped to a human use. Rural economy. Everything has its consequence. This is system too.

Rooks destroy their neighbors' nests in the beech-tops on the Hanger. Fallen nest-twigs kindle the fires of the poor. Rooks die in a freezing mist, wings iced together, and the poor eat well for a time.

Silk-wood abounds in the bogs. Beautiful bright chestnut color, soft and pliant. Women make besoms from it for the dusting of beds, curtains, carpets, and hangings.

Swan crashes into a window in Dorton. Sold to the miller at Hawkley. For pond or oven. Grass is dry, so the price of butter climbs and the taste of mutton improves. Farmers plant turnips everywhere now, even since I came into this country. So the flesh of wood pigeons loses its savor. Turnips abound, so lean sheep rise in value.

Oaks drop a heavy crop. Price of pigs goes up, barley down. Villagers drive barrow-hogs into the high-wood and onto the Hanger. They feed on beech-mast. Milch-sows eat yew-berries in the road, to their sorrow. Hogs graze on the stubbles, trouble the lanes, dig what truffles they can. Grub up the acorns that mice have buried one by one. Some years the hogs force their way into Mr. Gilbert White's outlet. Even to the ha-ha, before his people fall upon them with curses and cries.

The poor gather acorns too. Sell them for a shilling a

bushel. Selborne puts up its hogs to fatten in October. Killed and tubbed in January. Half a bushel of salt, two ounces of saltpeter, well-trod. Some years they die very good pork.

Holiburne truffler walks into Selborne. Two cur-dogs on a string. Sullen as himself. Searches hedges, coppices, hangers. Divides the truffles he finds, half to the landowner. For a shilling Mr. Gilbert White learns the art and mystery of truffling. But a shilling will not give him the nose he needs, nor bend it close enough to the ground. To those of us already down here, a truffle is an upwelling of musk. As plain as the July stench of jasmine that drives Mr. Gilbert White from his chamber. As dark as the pitch and tar on newly shorn sheep, depriving them of their old familiar smell, confusing the sense of kinship.

In summer, the Selborne people gather rushes in pastures and hedges and meadows. They strip them and soak them in bacon-pot scummings from January's pigs. Good clear light in the blackness. At the edges of day in the dark season. In kitchens and dairies.

Mr. Gilbert White conducts a systematic study of rush-making. A question of class. Careful wives of industrious laborers. Small farmers lighting their way. To nephew Samuel Barker: "Many gentlemen in Oxford had never heard of rushes; perhaps because they *were* gentlemen." The improvident poor burn halfpenny candles instead, which keeps them poor.

The considerable trees are assessed as items of human property. Mr. Gilbert White counts the trunks in the wood he owns. Ninety-four beeches, three ashes, two oaks in Sparrow's hanger. One beech of particular nobility, measured annually, girth and height.

A special attraction to trees that were planted by old men when they were mere boys. Sowed an acorn himself by the alcove when he was eleven. Now an oak four feet five inches around. He hews his beechen stock into planks. Has them plunged into Mr. James Knight's ponds, to be made into mangers.

The beeches on the Hanger belong to Magdalen College. And to whom does Magdalen College belong? Woodcutters fell the woods, strip by strip, year after year. Hanger dreadfully denuded. Wild strawberries spring up among the stumps, to be picked by children.

Even the wild cherries—the merry-trees—in the Great Mead have their use. Decoys. Drawing blackbirds to be shot by young Will Tanner. Saving thus the garden fruit.

The very stars have their numbers as well as names. A comet appears to Mr. Gilbert White not as an extravagant mystery, another incident in the annals of superstition, but as an eccentric manifestation in the constellation Aries. Beneath its twenty-fourth, twenty-ninth, and fifty-first stars, as listed in the English catalogue.

"Wonderful is the regularity observed by nature!" Mr. Gilbert White writes. Wonderful!

"Cleanly in all her ways." Cleanly!

"Seldom works in vain." Seldom!

And of all these things—stars, trees, pigs, twigs, prices, crops, people—I am easiest to number, being sole of my kind.

· · · · · ⌣

**W**eather is wild. Creatures that stay out of human reach. Wild is what the villagers haven't yet clutched to themselves. Beings that don't gather round to be touched at the sound of the feed-pail, the "sic, sic, sic" ing of the good-women after their pigs before they are put up a-fatting. Creatures that don't look up dog-like when they hear the word that means "look up at me."

Quail!

Mab!

Rover!

Fyfield!

*Timothy*!

But no place as wild as Selborne's single street. Nothing as wild as a pack of village boys. Scenting sixpences. Drowning in their own secretions. Breaking up the arch of a bricked grave merely to get at a wasps' nest. Beating down swallows stooping under the eaves. Twisting daws' nests out of the ground with forked sticks.

Even the very nieces and nephews of Mr. Gilbert White.

Scores of them. Considerate of my feelings. Easy with kidney-beans and cucumbers. Over-fond of the word "Timothy," perhaps. Even they destroy pheasants' nests while gathering strawberries in Goleigh Wood.

If the brute creation were wild in the human way, it would enter poor old Selborne, pull down the houses, and burn the hay-ricks. Foul the wells and nail farmers to the barn-ends.

Other creatures find their uses. Oxen are yoked and prodded, goad and word. Horses harnessed or saddled. Jumped and run and plowed. Dogs commanded and, as often, obeyed. Cats and ferrets set in stealth upon rats. Crickets lodged in paper houses and set chirping on sunny sills.

No one expects me to go a-mousing or a-ratting or to guard the flock or herd the neat-cattle. Nor to be fatted and killed like a pig. Or milked by dairy-maids out in pasture. Harnessed in draught. Set to lay. Warrened like rabbits. Caught and kept in a cage like a bullfinch or netted by larkers. Beat down by bat-fowlers or trapped on the downs like wheatears by shepherds. Run down by dogs and men on horseback. Dapped from the brook-head when mayflies mate. Shot on the wing and stuffed in a game pocket. Probed from my burrow with grass-stalks like the vanished race of field-crickets. Neither fleeced nor sheared. Not even anatomized and filed for reference.

And yet never let alone.

My true position? Abroad in the bean-field. Gone forever, it seems to the humans. "I should be very sorry to lose so old a domestic," Mr. Gilbert White writes, "that has behaved himself in so blameless a manner in the family for near fifty years."

Blameless footman. Worn-out cookmaid. Imbecile serving girl. Meek demeanor. Self-effacing behavior. Shuffle backward. Silent the door. Very bread in one's mouth not one's own.

"If attended to, it becomes an excellent weather-glass," the curate says of me. As if composing a notice of public sale. Blameless weather-glass. Domestic weather-glass. Self-dusting. Self-calibrating. Eats little. Long life. Accuracy guaranteed.

Shell worthless to humans, unlike the hawksbill's. Wrong calipash, wrong calipee. Waste too scant to spread on the garden. No song worth hearing. No skin worth tanning. No conversation worth taking down. No capers worth watching. Only the one autumnal trick, going underground, and the spring one, coming up again. And the other trick, of course. Longevity.

• • • • • ⌣

**H**eat of Cilicia in spring. Warm, spreading sea. Salt and light and stone. Expanse of time. Fit of place. That memory resides in my limbs. Hidden nearly all the year round by

Selborne's climate. The thought of it revives on the finest days. Carry myself from the damps of April—unseasonable snows, frost, and icicles—into the settled warmth of late May. All I can do. By then I begin to feel a nearly familiar ease. Summer established. Perfect summer.

These soft Selborne mornings. Languid heat already in air. The well sinks. Martins gather loam in Gracious Street for their houses. Bantam hen brings out her chicks in ostentatious pride. Mr. Gilbert White takes note of all these things. Measures the rain. Brings his balance forward. And he takes note of me. I occupy a corner of his eye whenever he is in the garden. Always conscious, this time of year, of that first escape.

I watch him watching me. Sometimes he even seems aware of being watched. Looks up from sowing a crop of parsnips. Cutting a bottle-nosed cantaloupe. Finds me musing nearby, as if I were an unexpected melon just now ripening on the vine. Look of consciousness crosses his face. Awareness of my awareness.

Thousands of pairs of eyes in this garden. Few of them able to make a human feel looked at. Strangely impervious to the level gaze of a swallow or a bumble bee. No natural predators. Unaware of the menace in a hedgehog's glare. Blind to the query in a bantam's eye. Few creatures cast their wishes into a look. Those alone catch a human's notice. Rover. Fyfield. The parlor-cat. The one wise sow. Irritable gander. Milch-cow. Saddle-mare.

Mr. Gilbert White watches me watching him. My gaze is as weightless upon him as the shadow of a moth. He feels it anyway.

Rare the human who bestows his confidence upon a tortoise. One occupant of Earth to another. To acquit a reptile of an insuperable difference in breeding. Unforgivable difference in kind.

The sufferings of my solitude Mr. Gilbert White plainly feels. My hermit-like condition. But it is a mammal's conception of solitude. I was laid in solitude, hatched in solitude, all but conceived in solitude. "One of the first great dictates of nature," Mr. Gilbert White notes of maternal affection. But it is only as strong as the helplessness of the newborn. Humans at one extreme. Tortoises at the other.

And is he not feeling for himself? A man essentially solitary among so much kin, so many friends? So close to nature that only he knows how removed from nature he really is?

The truth of my time among humans. As subject to their neglect, their forgetfulness, their most trivial intentions, as I am to their malice. As vulnerable to their wonder as their loathing.

Set loose in the garden, now these dozen years ago. The country people quickly judge whether I concern them or not. Their habit in most things. Practical breed. Not their business, they decide. A gentry affair. One of the curate's whims, like the board-statue of the great ruddy Greek at the foot of the Hanger. Better for a coaching-inn sign than to stand at the edge of the woods, staring at one.

I make no sense to Goody Hammond. No more than the sundial at the edge of the ha-ha. But I am as much a fact. Not to be denied. No surprise in my continued presence, day after day.

Now and then a naturalist—rare as a merganser—descends upon the village. A feast of observation for Mr. Gilbert White. Company of his own particular kind. They walk the parish together. "No bird, plant, or insect came before them unascertain'd," he writes.

The naturalists appraise me. Turn me over in their minds. They would like to ascertain the hinges of my being. Have me out of myself. Find my cognomen—my synonym—in the Linnaean system. Myself unnecessary once the Latin name is found. They would like to answer the question of my prolonged existence. As if it were not implicit in theirs as well.

But in the end, they consider, I am alien to this district. Visiting from nowhere. No notion what place I am fitted to. Vagabond on this soil. A condition with no meaning to a naturalist. Subject to a certain disregard therefore. Less instructive than the merest mole-cricket churring by night here in the land of its ancestors.

I worry visitors even now. Country lad spreading black-smith's cinders in the crocus and vine-beds under the dining-room window. Struck dumb by the venom of my appearance. Shovel in a brawny hand. Forearm like oak. Forehead too. Dangerous creature. My shell silently absorbs me. Where best to strike the beast? Saint George wonders. To strike at all?

Thomas taps the window-glass. Spell broken. Entirely his fault, Thomas says. Forgot to mention me. Steps outside. Sets me among the larkspurs across the walk. Word of further explanation to the country lad. The humans glance in my direction. I give them nothing to see.

Some of the vicarage ladies—Mrs. Etty's sisters come to visit—enjoy the thought of shuddering at the thought of me. Parade through the garden once or twice a year. Trailing fingers over the blossoms. Massaging the apricots, devouring the currants. If they were blackbirds they would be shot. Drowned in treacle if wasps.

The vicarage ladies lack Mr. Gilbert White's diverse taste in nature. Tolerate the winged creation as long as it keeps its distance. Swan on a still pond. Nightingale in the French-mere. Chicken in a fricassee. Accept the existence of quadrupeds with hair or fur. Necessary creatures after all. Conveyance. Wool. Joints of meat. Reptiles entirely superfluous.

A wonder that these ladies consent to inhabit their own flesh. What edifice is this delicacy the peak of? How do their cucumbers grow? Mrs. Rebecca Snooke was of sterner stuff.

The vicarage arrives. I am set out of the way among the

artichokes, where the ladies are not likely to venture. Still, they worry that I will rush at their ankles.

A mild suspicion of humans grows upon Mr. Gilbert White. The worst of their character so often prevails. Religion and the study of nature teach him to think it. Professional intimacy with parishioners. Not prone to confession, but they do confide. Will misbehave. Drunken farmer bawls in the street before carrying his new bride— bawling too—out of Selborne. Royal Navy kidnaps a carter's boy in an ale-house and hauls him off to sea. Paralytic strangles himself with a leathern thong. London crowds riot. French crowds behead their anointed king.

And vicarage ladies will bruise wall fruit. Boys will torment squirrels. Never mind the unspeakable temptation of a tortoise to young scholars.

"There is too strong a propensity in human nature towards persecuting and destroying!" Mr. Gilbert White writes.

The rest of nature concurs.

〜 • • • • •

**M**rs. Rebecca Snooke was not inclined to pick me up. Mr. Henry Snooke soiled his hands with me just once, the day of my arrival. Set me down upon the ground and then looked for somewhere to wipe his hands. As if I oozed. Gardener's assistant teased a pretty young maid with me one summer morning. Tried to embosom me upon her. End of his duties in that household. She followed him out of the parish, midriff swelling, not long after.

Then comes a pleasant morning in August 1775. Mr. Gilbert White, visiting his aunt. I hear him searching the courtyard beds. Never a long search. Find the hepatica, find the tortoise. Leaves above me part. He takes me up in his hands. Closes me in a wicker basket lined with moss. Years since I was last picked up, much less basketed.

Out the gate with me under his arm. The first time I've stirred beyond these walls since I was deposited within them. Thirty-five years without a glimpse of the greater world. I peer at Ringmer through a slit between the basket-ribs. Down the hill toward the village center. Through a door. Bell jangles overhead.

Mr. Gilbert White opens the basket. Before I can glance about me, he lifts me into the pan of a shop-scale. Hanging over a wooden counter. High above a stone floor. I step out of the pan and onto the counter. Mr. Gilbert White catches me and sets me in the pan again. But this time—*on my back!*

I do what any tortoise would. Curtail myself. It is the power of being a tortoise. Legs, head, all but the least nub of my tail vanish. Shopkeeper fiddles with the scales, which want to swing. "Six pounds, three-quarters, and one ounce!" he announces. Mr. Gilbert White scribbles on a piece of paper.

Crowd of humans standing around him—where did they come from?—roars with laughter. Shop suddenly fills with the brawling of human breath. A close, sulfurous braying.

"A pennyworth, Richard, of the old Sussex tortoise!" comes a shout. As though I were a tobacco or malted barley. More laughter. One human wonders aloud what I'm worth in the king's coin. Whorled stub of a filthy finger, dank with the fundament-scent—the basso of its owner's body— reaches inside the head-shield of my carapace. Some village Polyphemus, already blinded, searching for No Man.

Mr. Gilbert White gently replaces me in the basket— upright—and closes the lid.

Six pounds thirteen ounces. Shopkeeper's figures are wrong by the immeasurable weight of my fears. I thought it was the soup for me at last.

I blame Mrs. Rebecca Snooke for allowing the weighing. But I blame Mr. Gilbert White for the project. Insatiable curiosity. Extravagant wonder. Not the least assuaged by the consolations of his religion. And I blame him, far worse, for laying me on my back. My safety in mind, perhaps. Perhaps only the shopkeeper's convenience—a misplaced hope that I wouldn't void my fears in the scale.

But in his desire to learn that I weigh six pounds thirteen ounces on the 7th of August 1775, Mr. Gilbert White violates the inflexible law of uprightness. Bad enough to pick me up. But he turns me over as though upside down were merely the left hand of right side up. There is only one posture to a land-tortoise. Four feet square on the ground. Just as there is one orbit to Earth. One heaven on a Selborne sabbath morning.

"It was never weighed before," Mr. Gilbert White notes, "but seems to be much grown since it came." Much grown and much wiser. Student of human nature, even then, after thirty-five years among them. Student of myself, in my red-brick prison. Student of circumstance.

"Pray let it be weighed every year," says one of Mr. Gilbert White's brothers.

· · · · · ⌒

**S**o it has been ever since. Twice a year I am a tortoise hung in a needy shop, as the poet says. Spring sun warms my carapace at last. Two days out of my winter's nest, and I find myself lifted from the grass. Autumn withers. Nearly time to dig. I await what's coming. Carried over Selborne street, past the butcher's. Across the Plestor and through the door of Mr. Jack Burbey's shop. Suspended on my back in the scales above the counter. Like a cheese indifferent to up or down.

Village boys crow like cockerels during the procession. Shopkeeper slips a cabbage leaf in the weighing pan first. Waits a moment or two, while I ease myself, before he tries to balance the scales.

I have learned to be still. To trust Mr. Gilbert White.

# Timothy

Never glance at the soot-darkened ceiling, the clutter of parcels and boxes and ribbons. The nostrums and salts. The ledgers and rows of drawers and small jars. Keep my nostrils as tightly closed as my eyes. Can't stop my ears to the boys' cheering.

I presume that there will be no horror. None beyond lifting, carrying, prodigious height, curious rabble, inversion, and the return journey across the street, through the stable-yard, and back to the garden. No soup and no slip. Only the greatest care in handling me.

In thirteen years I have never been dropped among the boys' swift feet. Never kicked head over tail. Never rolled through the village along my equator. Chased by dogs down Gracious Street or Huckers Lane. I have merely been stood on my back. Rocking side to side like a beached coracle.

The meager harvest of those outings? The knowledge that my weight rises or falls by an ounce or two, as I feast or abstain, but scarcely at all over the years. Therefore, as Mr. Gilbert White notes, "these reptiles do not, as some have imagined, continue to grow as long as they live."

Therefore, indeed. Consider the carapace. Even at hatching I was no formless spawn. No Selborne infant able to grow which-a-way without stopping. What other imaginings will Mr. Gilbert White refute at my expense?

He picks me up one day in Ringmer. Idle question on his face. Feels my tail and feet and as much of my neck as I allow. Concludes that I have no perceptible pulse. As if I would keep my pulse where a human could touch it. What would be the point of all this armor then?

He forgets how discomfiting the incandescence of mammals feels to a reptile. Their abruptness. The velocity of their existence. To live such long lives at such terrible speed. And to get no further than if they had lived more slowly.

In Selborne he strides down to the bee-stalls beside the Balm of Gilead tree. Carries his father's speaking-trumpet, purchased in 1757. Lifts the narrow end to his lips and bellows at the hive. "With such an exertion of voice," he writes, "as would have hailed a ship at the distance of a mile."

Gleaners down the Ewell look up from the corn. Men at the hop-kilns pause. A naturalist, they know, is half a fool. Still, the curate notes, the bees "pursued their various employments undisturbed, and without showing the least sensibility or resentment." Who is the more rational in this case? The insect or the parson?

Mr. Gilbert White approaches me with the same five-shilling instrument. Aims the bell of the trumpet into the laurel hedge. Sharp intake of breath. Cries out my name, as if expecting my shell to return the echo. I react much as the bees do. Not the least sensibility or resentment. Best response to a naturalist. Let him form what conclusions he may. Any reaction only raises new questions.

The curate confesses to frequent returns of deafness, coming on for many years. Now the villagers bellow at him.

Trumpet in earnest. Rural sounds lost to him at times. Intimations. His neighbors hear the firing during the great review at Bagshot Heath. Mr. Gilbert White does not. Though news of it wakes pleasant memories of a review he witnessed half a life earlier.

Thomas listens alone now for the Portsmouth evening gun. Mr. Gilbert White waits to feel it in his bones. Thomas harks to the stone-curlews on their way to the uplands when he rises in the dark to brew. Reports their passing to his master. Who jots down the fact.

Is it not enough to shout in my ear? Mr. Gilbert White chronicles my liking for endive and gooseberry. How I hold back the outer leaves of a Coss lettuce with my feet. Examines my excrement. Discerns that I urine plentifully, emitting a chalk-like substance, like a bird of prey. Who is privy to such matters among humans? Who surveys among them what he calls the "consequences of eating"?

One more hypothesis remains to be tested. The amphibian one. Arid, my shell. Arid, my hide. Arid, my very manner. And yet a man of system must not *suppose* that I am a native of dry land. Even though he *supposes* that I am lonely.

Amphibious tortoises do exist. Mr. John White saw them in Andalusia. Dr. Richard Chandler, vicar of the neighboring parish of East Worldham, has seen them in the Levant. William Derham—the physico-theologist—asserts that the tortoise is an amphibious animal. A footnote of his great work. The assertion looms over Mr. Gilbert White. *Physico-*

*Theology*, after all, *Or, A Demonstration of the Being and Attributes of God, from His Works of Creation*.

Yet there is such "a propensity in mankind towards deceiving and being deceived," Mr. Gilbert White cautions, "that one cannot safely relate any thing from common report, especially in print, without expressing some degree of doubt and suspicion."

Therefore better to try the question. Perhaps the curate wanted to try it years before, in Ringmer. There, in a backward spring, in that brick-lined swamp, I was nearly amphibious by force. Perhaps he was prevented by Mrs. Rebecca Snooke. She can stop nothing now.

In the company of Dr. Richard Chandler—that prattling cock-bird—the time comes at last. July of my first summer in Selborne. Soft gray day. A Sunday. Clerics at large in the afternoon.

"We put Timothy into a tub of water," Mr. Gilbert White notes, "& found that he sank gradually, & walked on the bottom of the tub; he seemed quite out of his element & was much dismayed. This species seems not at all amphibious."

Footnote refuted!

His is a narrow account of the incident. Terseness expressing a naturalist's shame? Dismay at his doings? Far unequal to mine. "This species seems not at all amphibious!" Bold conclusion of a brave venture!

My legs begin to windmill over the water-tub. Rainwater closes round me. Loggerheads of that ancient coast slipping joyously into the sea. Shells disappearing beneath the foam. They are nowhere to be seen. The memory seems almost shaming in the circumstances.

I am not taken in by the tide, borne up by the counterpoise of the deep. I sink. The water doesn't sustain or welcome me. It soaks me like a week's worth of washing. I am merely a long-pampered tortoise—decades removed from my natural life—standing on the bottom of a water-tub in the south of England. Two male humans in wigs look down with expectant, distorted faces. Waiting to draw the proper inference from my unhappiness.

Next day they weigh me, and my unhappiness is complete.

· · · · · ～

**M**r. Gilbert White's house looms hard against the village street. Cliff-like, muting the street-sounds. As solid in appearance as the rock-like clouds crowding a late-spring sky. Roof-tiles on the gables glower in the rain—the color of impending thunder. Here Mr. Gilbert White does the business of living.

What opacity there is in his character, I attribute to the sturdy walls of his domicile. He probes closely into the conduct and manners of every being in his parish. Yet lives largely hidden from their sight. Like the swift, he "cannot be so narrowly watched as those species that build more openly." No creature excels the human in matters of nidification.

Mr. Gilbert White arrives on horseback from Newton Valence, late at night, and retires. Makes his way through the dark house with the aid of a rush-light. Dim glow passing from room to room, window to window. Up stairs into the bedroom over the kitchen. Then out.

If he stirs too often in bed, he steps down again and outside into the darkness to find Jupiter or Saturn. Sometimes through the parlor door. Sometimes through the kitchen. To consider the Dipper. To see how the moon is waning, where the glass stands. To visit, if the night is warm, the necessary-house hidden behind a screen of laurels. But then always inside and up to bed again.

Summer means cantaloupe-parties or tea. In the Hermitage high on the Hanger. A strong, substantial cot, well-thatched. Above the zigzag path from the foot of the Pound Field. Large white cross to catch the eye. Sweet afternoons above Selborne. Company of kin and neighbors. Succulence of melons, acerbity of tea. Set apart from all that labor in the world below. Lifted above one's cares. London somewhere off in the distance. Brother Benjamin White's roomy shop. Horace's Head, 51 Fleet Street. Old men in leathern doublets at the press.

Sometimes the hermit appears. Hairy gown, rosary beads, conical hat, rude belt. A Hampshire Crusoe. Unmistakable features of a sibling White. Wise but gaily anti-social. Self-contained for ten or fifteen minutes. Ascetic until the sandwiches. Not quite the prophetic strain. Flirtatious. Happy to startle the ladies. Gothic fright. Impersonating a mammal's notion of solitude. Amused by his own gravity. The mild utterance of a minor poet.

Even now the Hermitage recalls the days, long ago, when twenty at a time might crowd its shelter. Female visitors from the vicarage. Dressed as shepherds and shepherdesses. Much to the confusion of actual shepherds who watch the good folk climb the zigzag path. Once in the afternoon and again by lamplight.

A tent below the Hanger. In those days. Striped pavilion at the crest of the Short Lythe. Mrs. Etty and her maidens. Those sweet fields. Walking down the village to Mr. Gilbert White's house "to be electrified in the evening." Mr. Thomas White's electrical machine. Brother John also an Electrician. Hair standing on end.

That fashion has passed. That youth. Tents folded. Ladies soundly married. No more electrifying. The machine is merely another weather device now. Shoots fierce sparks, rings bells, when a summer storm gathers near Lambeth.

Tea-party, cantaloupe-party. Down the Hanger before darkness. Down the Zigzag into a deeper twilight. Night clotting in the lowlands. Along the brick-walk. Welcome of the house. Lights within. Echo of its walls. Comfort of the fire, candles, parlor. Society of Mrs. John White.

Letters to write, a note in the journal. What blooms.

What rain falls. What the glass did. How the wind quarters. Whether the hops run out their poles. If the hay is making. Quiet stitching of time.

Rural sounds almost never cease in June and July. Voices of yeomen in the nearby fields. Words that drive the horses. Slap of leather against wood and flesh. Iron against iron and earth. Bells in the fields. St. Mary's open-mouthed ring floods the valley. Human enterprise is as wide as the sun's arc. Here in the north where the light scarcely dies. Selborne waits until late to withdraw into its brief midsummer sleep.

Male glow-worms follow the candle-light into Mr. Gilbert White's parlor. I approach the glimmer. It spills through open windows. Under the flycatcher's nest in the vines, out onto the grass. Flickering as moonlight never does, catching the silhouettes of humans within.

Copper cowl to the parlor chimney. Flock satin paper on the walls. Italian veined marble. Fine stout Turkey carpet. Bought of Joseph Luck at the Original Carpet Warehouse— Bread Street, Cheapside—in the week before Mrs. Rebecca Snooke's death. Lively clatter of kin in such comfortable surroundings—nephews, nieces, brothers, sisters.

Visitors crowd the months of summer and early autumn. Appraising the changes in each other. In the garden. In the neighborhood. Some seek me out on the instant for a private interlude. Unchanged they find me. Themselves as variable as always. Some fit only for reading aloud at evening. Some sing, some sit silent. Some—the nieces—play elegant lessons upon Mrs. Etty's harpsichord, borrowed for the occasion.

Brittle notes swarm over the window-case. Ants across a well-polished table-top. Ordering and disordering themselves before expiring, reordered, in the night air. Their importunate echoes haunt Mr. Gilbert White as he wakes in the mornings. Deranging his meditations.

Too clever, too mannered, this remembered music. Lacking, in memory, even the scant body of the instrument's voice. The complications of an inanimate box. Mr. Gilbert White's true music is the repeated, unresolved music of birdsong. Melody that never finds the tonic again. Resolved only in the being that utters it. Still air that absorbs it. Season that prompts it.

I listen, haunted too. Sometimes I hear the music nearby. Just under the Portland sill. Other times I hear it from farther off. Where it fades into the hedges. Less substantial than the scent of the wind.

And in that music—little as it is—there is all the elaboration these humans are capable of. Order and disorder. Ornament and element. Ruck of their lives, jumbled together. Weaving and interweaving in a curious succession. Night's animals taking place of day's. Rows of house-fronts and roof-tops. Embroidery of the plantings in this garden. Passion-flowers beside the curate's street-front door. Courtesies of speech. All the regularity of this irregular species.

〜 . . . . .

The evening damp has still not fallen. The air elastic yet. Young people enter the garden, leaving grave folks round the chimney. Pleased to think themselves grave and old before such an early fire. Age is not intolerable if your shins are warm.

The young ones whisper in the out-of-doors. They feel its presence. On the grass-plot. Beyond the ha-ha. Hushed by the twilight. These cousins. So confidential, so surprised to be grown. So manly and womanly, so come to adulthood. So conscious. Weight of one another's presence. Saturation of being. Grass pulsing in the night-breeze all around them.

Put out at nurse in Selborne, one by one. At the teat of some village goodwoman. Suckling on the Hanger. In the coppices. Carried through the street on a morning errand. Across the fields to bring beer to the reapers. Fastened to a moist dug with a glutinous mouth. Breast seeping like the climate of this Selborne. Thin drool down the infant's chin. What a wet species it is! Entire village at suck.

Molly White's Benjamin now a thrashing young brat. Taught to say "Timothy" when held out before me. Partial to roasted apples and the engravings on Mr. Gilbert White's wainscot. As helpless, as incapable, as a new-pipped cuckoo or squab-young stolen from a swift's nest. Even in his second and third summers. Entirely dependent on the vigilance of others. Prior arrangement of instinct. Very sure of that vigilance they are, these humans. Such is the power of instinct. Let it lapse in a single generation, and that is the end of this species, for all its talk of reason and faith.

Through the wicket-gate, onto the grass-walk and down the outlet they go. Among the maple hedges. Young of this human brood. As graceful as the vertical ever get, leaning on each other's arms. Display of kinship. A solemn bond, and yet not nearly as tight as a flock of swallows on the wing. They walk deep into the night-shadows. At a mating age, but mating curiously postponed.

Somber, joyful mass of the Hanger blockading the low southern stars. As though it were kin as well. Sheep-down beyond its brow like a small sky of grass. An inexplicable kindness to that precipice of chalk, its woods and rooks. White poplar at the foot of the Bostal. Path cut along the slope in my first Selborne autumn. Troops of laborers, spades in hand. Pyrites in the clay, ammonites in the chalk as they dig. Gradual romantic walk up the face of the hill. For horses and heifers and humans not equal to the Zigzag straight up the side.

Looming in summer. Withdrawing in winter. Height of Venus measured against the Hanger. Hour by hour shifts in the greening of spring. Beautiful rimes. Picturesque tinges. Autumnal scenes. Most lovely lights and shades.

Birds' eggs and nests, acorns and berries. Smooth grotesque bark of the oldest beeches. Fetid hellebores in the undergrowth. Orchids and periwinkle and gentian. Whole childhoods hidden in its shade.

Ravens and thistle-down launch from its heights. Wind-hovers and wood-owls nest in its boughs. Villagers peer down through the beech-leaves onto their own habitations.

Good glazed stone and brick cottages. Chambers above stairs. Hop gardens sheltered by hedges. Small bleached fields of wheat. Oats. Barley. Sainfoin. Turnips. Gardens, enclosures. A rustic patchwork. Smoke that rises when brush burns, when lime-kilns fire, when winter comes. Sun-reek from the garden walks and roofs. Pasture-corners crowded with sheep, gathering like evening fog. Every rod under cultivation or care. The course of their own lives, from thatch-eave to grave.

Yet how the nephews and nieces (and their uncles!) love to shout from the top of the Hanger. Village and Lythe return the echo. They halloo just to see who responds.

"*Tityre, tu patulae recubans* . . . ," comes the cry from a steep balk above a hollow lane at the top of the King's Field. "*Tityre, tu patulae recubans* . . . ," answers the Galley-lane hop-kiln, able to repeat ten dactylic syllables without fault.

Mr. Edmund White, one of the nephews, comes over on an August evening. From Newton Valence, just beyond the top of the down. Fires his swivel-guns from Baker's Hill, then from the alcove. Sounds a third salvo from the Hermitage, to the satisfaction of all.

"The repercussions & echoes delighted the hearers,"

reports Mr. Gilbert White, "not only filling the Lythe with the roar, as if all the beeches were tearing-up by the roots; but turning to the left they pervaded the vale above Combwood-ponds; & after a pause seemed to take-up the crash again, & to extend round Hartley-hangers; & to die away at last among the coppices, & coverts of Wardle-ham."

The kin of this house revel in noise as much as they revel in quiet. Greet Five November with Roman candles, serpents, and sky rockets. The memory of that ancient, unacquitted betrayal. Popish treachery. Sheep appointed to the slaughter. Glee of the entire street. Detonations. Sudden flares and hissings.

Horses stare. Trot round the paddocks in their most significant manner. Dogs lie low. Fyfield cries most mournfully. Nothing now frights me in the way of noise. Constant alarums. Greenfinch in the polyanths! Blackbird in the cherry tree! Papist in the cellar, all those years ago!

The whole of Selborne slumbers under the stars. All but the creatures that nest below ground or in the cavities of rocks and trees. Sheep lie abroad around the village by night. So do cattle and, in summer, horses. Hogs doze among beech-roots and in autumn thickets. Hollows sculpted to fit their bodies. These creatures—domestic as humans—lie out every night in the darkness. No less composure than during the day. Night is home to them too. A soft thatch of clouds pulled apart by the breeze.

Old woman living at the foot of the Hanger. She curls up

in a hedge-hollow. By an ash within sight of the common. Gypsy girl under a blanket. Giving birth in a September deluge. Circumstances too trying for a cow, the curate notes. Boy dozes beside his dog while watching the flocks on the sheep-down. Impoverished wanderer sleeps against a rick of cow-grass. Fleeing his own parish. Barely sleeps, hoping to wake before the farmer does, who rises well before first light.

Even in summer I withdraw by four o'clock in the afternoon. Only a seeming withdrawal. Rouse again and again throughout the night. After forty years in a red-brick box, my waking is not as wary as it once was. This garden, too, is unnaturally safe. I try to keep the old ways that all creatures keep. One eye open. Skin listening. Not in fear but attention.

Curlew clamors in the dark. Night-moth agitates in the air above me. Sly predation of village cats. Dog come to eat gooseberries ripe from the hedge. Piping note of young fern-owls in the distance. Chattering of their elders, like the noise of a razor-grinder's wheel on the street. Chirping of the grasshopper lark. Wood-owls hooting from the walnut tree overhead. Singing of wood-larks. Churring of mole-crickets. Stirring of cattle in the grass. Bat a-flutter low along the fruit-wall. Lonely pace of a traveler's horse making its way down Selborne toward The Compasses in the dark. Sounds of dreaming, as the humans in this village toss in their beds.

## Timothy

I attend to the shadows. To the night-shapes of the trees surrounding this garden. Thatched bulk of houses down the village-back. I cannot hear everything the foxes hear or smell everything the dogs smell or fear everything the humans fear. But I can sense the remote static of the aurora borealis stretching east to west across the welkin. Feel the stars overhead when the wind drops. Resonant in their silence. Smell the dawn when it is still just a premonition. A stirring in the throat of the earliest songbird. The wakeful rooster.

Never has Mr. Gilbert White slept the night out of doors. Even under a tent in the Great Mead. Even on the finest of midsummer eves. He always chooses to sleep within. A plaster ceiling, timbers, and tiles over his dreams. Meanwhile the white-thorn near the ash-house glows on moon-shiny nights. Full of blossom.

・ ・ ・ ・ ・ ⌒

**A**uthor of the great *Methodus*, Mr. John Ray, asks, "Why should there be implanted in each Sex such a vehement, an inexpugnable Appetite of Copulation?" Mr. John Ray's wife knew full well why. Locked in a despairing embrace. Wishing her husband could wait with such a question. The earth would soon empty without such vehement, inexpugnable promptings. A stirring gratification for thinking ahead. Even when one is not thinking ahead at all.

The rub and thump of mating rouses the parish in spring. Restless pairings, quick conjugations. Overspill of seed. Coop, stable, sty, and fold. The fevered opportunity of every encounter. Tups and ewes in neighboring fields. At it. Treading of birds on the nest. In the trees, on the ground, in the garden and sky. Adhesion of frogs. Earthworms laid end to end, hermaphroditic.

Mr. Gilbert White listens with maiden ears. Mrs. John White with the ears of the bride. She from a broken pairing. He, like me, unpaired.

To his nephew Mr. Samuel Barker, the curate writes, "You are not the only person that finds himself under difficulties respecting the sexuality of mosses." Sends along edifying illustrations.

"In the plate respecting the male and female *Vallisneria*," he observes, "you will see a wonderful instance of the wisdom of providence."

Other creatures have wonderful instances too. No less mysterious than those of the mosses. Consider the eel. Consider the reptiles.

"There is a degree of dubiousness and obscurity," Mr. Gilbert White notes, "attending the propagation of this class of animals."

Though to a reptile, it is plain as day. No more obscure than the propagation of humans. Vastly less dubious, since the question of costume—getting into or out of in a timely fashion—never arises. None of the passion for privacy. No

pretense of fidelity beyond the enormous fidelity of copulation. Never the ruddiness of shame or guilt that humans
display over the nature of the act itself. Virtuosos of despair
and justification. No need to credit the wisdom of providence. Wisdom aplenty in the flesh.

Wisdom in its season. Birds set aside what the curate
calls the "soft passion" in winter. Worms defer to the frost.
Every being reserves a part of the year for propagating. All
but humans. Conceiving and whelping in every week of the
calendar. In and out of wedlock, in and out of doors. In ash-
house, barn, and bedchamber. Wherever the fancy takes
them.

Reason, Mr. Gilbert White writes, "would often vary and
do that by many methods which *instinct* effects by one alone."

True in the matter of mating too. A behavior unfet-
tered in humans. The intercourse of reasonable beings.
Simplicity of instinct embroidered by lust. Variations,
etudes, improvisations. I suspect that humans of breeding
age can copulate from almost any direction.

An agility matched only by their haste. Rush to coitus.
And to an end to coitus. Curious in creatures so endowed
with time. The naturalist mocks the composure of tortoises—"an animal," Mr. Gilbert White notes, "said to be a
whole month in performing one feat of copulation." Propor-
tioning one's industry to one's pleasures. *Feat* only in
human eyes.

Dubious and obscure the propagation of humans.
Witness Goody Hammond.

"This is the person that Thomas says he likes as well as a man." Mr. Gilbert White to Molly White. "And indeed excepting that she wears petticoats, and now and then has a child, you would think her a man."

Excepting, indeed. And excepting wings, beak, and a pair of bandy legs, I am a kingfisher. Thomas likes Goody Hammond for her self-absorbing labors. Not for what she does or doesn't resemble. Bare-armed Amazon with a hedge-hook for a bow.

Fashionable women visiting from London. To Lord Stawel at Alice Holt. Strolling the village, arm in arm. Touring this garden. Nothing ambiguous in their markings. Sexual compasses flaunted with clothing. A separate species from Goody Hammond, separate even from Mrs. John White. Flounced and bedizened and most woefully over-hatted. Ostrich plumes ride up and down on their heads as they walk. Curious virility in dress. Ingenious contrivance. How do their males come at them? And at what cost?

Mr. Gilbert White takes the rut for granted in others. Never confesses to the appetite in himself. Pushed copulation to the side of his plate as a young man. Restrained by his college, his calling. Penalties laid upon the Oxford man who weds. Loss of fellowship. Withdrawn from the fray that surrounds him. Decorum of his station in life, though it hardly deters others in his garb. Economy stronger than the sex within him.

Considerable expenses of the household. Erecting the

great parlor. Cost of the garden. Blacksmith's bills. Six hundred building bricks. Twenty bushels of gray lime. Price of a neat post-chaise hired from Mr. Harrow. Six shillings threepence from Selborne to Alton, every trip. And back again. Purchase of adjoining gardens, strips of land, and the fields behind the house. Calendar year of butcher's meat, straw, and oats. Matter of £34 and some shillings one year, £47 another. "I say received in full by me. John Hale"—and signed for year after year. Mr. Richard Knight's malt. Farmer Hale's malt. Suit of clothes from Bunce the tailor. Farmer Berriman for plowing the Ewel-close. Carriage of a hogshead of port wine from Southampton.

And those twenty-four blue plates and egg cups? The eighteen London ivory-handled knives and forks from Adey Bellamy facing Grocers Alley in the Poultry?

Impediments many. Incentives few. Three-score nieces and nephews. Plenty of young people. And now in the household Mrs. John White. Sister, companion, friend. All the family a man could desire. More than enough intercourse in the purview of St. Mary's. Licit and otherwise. No need to add his mite.

．．．．．〜

In spring the parish swims in the airborne milt of its vegetation. Clouds of male yew farina on the drift. St. Mary's. Accidental abundance of male yews in the churchyards, the curate notes. "Since men, when they first planted yews, little dreamed that there were sexes in trees." Less concupiscent trees in the churchyards had they known. Less apt to dust parishioners in pollen.

In the hop-grounds, farmers cultivate the female hops. Males rooted out wherever they appear. As if the vines were cattle and only the cows were wanted. But something is lacking without the male.

"Male plants will not bear good hops," Mr. Gilbert White observes. After much thought he wonders, "But may not some of their farina be necessary towards rendering the female productions more perfect?" That question he puts to his neighbors. The female productions improve.

Hops all across the parish. Hedged and gardened over the south of England. A canopy of vines on the chestnut poles. Bitter cones picked and dried and bagged. Hop-kilns kindled after the picking. Effluvial perfume of fading summer. Bags and bags in wagon-loads to Weyhill Fair. The wonder is not that humans manage to propagate the crop. The wonder is that they manage to propagate themselves.

A neighboring cleric believes that a bachelor is unable to recognize swallows. Little-noted advantage of the wedded state. So incomplete, so traditional, is the notion of sexual system. Was there a time when humans put males to death because they bore no children? How have they kept from caponizing each other?

But instinct teaches what reason learns too late, even

among humans. At least in this most instinctive of matters. Sap rises. Dew gathers. In the promiscuity of nature each finds its own.

The sportsman knows the cock pheasant the instant it flushes. Hunter kens the dog-fox on open ground. Poacher feels the roe-swelling of the trout in Dorton stream. The leisurely Mrs. John Mulso tells the bull from the milch-cow by the hump on his shoulder. No need to inspect the apparatus. She knows the hen by its petticoat. Not by the lack of comb or crow alone.

The good farmer is quick with the knife. Wethers and oxen, not rams and bulls. Only enough seed to go around is wanted. One cock too many balds the hens. Peace in the barnyard.

"Castration has a strange effect," Mr. Gilbert White notes. Shrinking the gulf between the sexes. The gelding. The barrow. The capon. The spayed sow, cut by the man who makes that his trade. So the world is ordered. Old Noah's method, two by two. Male and female. And the barnyard sex in between.

But Mr. Gilbert White, the naturalist, sexes every creature. Mr. and Mrs. Flea. Mole-cricket and his courtesan. Harems of the avian tribe. The harvest-mouse at nurse. Male from female, youth from adult, mating from non-mating, species from species. Peering at the particulars. The nest. The song. The sex-dance. The inevitable union.

He chooses his time. Mid-April. He watches closely the

short-winged summer birds. Before the beeches open. Before the white-thorn hedges thicken with blossom. The characteristic manner of every bird. Swagger of crows and daws afoot. Bank martin's wriggling, desultory flight. The languishing, faltering greenfinch in love.

Only those who conceal their amorous intrigues deceive the curate. Who do not court on the ground like rooks. Or shriek in juncture on the wing like swifts. Or certify before the altar at least some of their copulations, like humans.

Mr. Gilbert White sexes everything except the months and seasons themselves. Everything but the weather and the ingredients in the landscape.

And of those he says, "I think there is somewhat peculiarly sweet and amusing in the shapely figured aspect of chalk-hills in preference to those of stone, which are rugged, broken, abrupt, and shapeless."

◠ • • • • •

Spring runs ahead of itself. Into the heat of late May. Selborne fair convenes. A cattle-mart. The Plestor crowded with bawling and lowing. Bellowing of humans drunk on housekeepers' beer, brewed specially for the fair. Reaching to where I lie in the beans and the sainfoin—hidden without hiding.

Great storm of June comes on. Sulfurous blue mist along the sloping woods. Rushing and roaring of hail. Then, at last, a settled month. Pleasant breezes, fine gleams, red evenings. Golden weather. High summer of that *annus mirabilis*, the human year 1784.

Mr. Charles Etty returns from the sea. Trim young man, suitable size for the ship-board life. Dwarfed by Molly White, like his mother, Mrs. Andrew Etty. First visit to Selborne since the death of his father, the vicar, in the backward spring of the year. Delirious fever and blains. Snow thick upon the village in April. Deep as a horse's belly along the hedges. Poor-tax doubled.

As late as I've ever risen here. The Reverend Andrew Etty, B.D., already laid to earth. Conjugal, parental, sacerdotal virtues combined, a preacher of righteousness. In his vicarage-chimney Mr. Gilbert White's flitch of bacon often hung to dry.

Voyage of the *Duke of Kingston*. Mr. Andrew Etty's ship. Burnt by accident off Ceylon. Mr. Andrew Etty takes passage aboard the man-of-war *Exeter*. Madagascar, Isle of Ascension. Ship so crazed that it was broken up and burned at the Cape of Good Hope. Young man at last embarks for London aboard the transport *Content*.

His cargo? Hummingbirds shot at the Cape, ostrich eggs, turtle eggs, fine shells, a curious cudweed from a Dutchman's garden. The pinnacle of this sailor's small virtù? Two finely checkered tortoises—live—from Madagascar. Prizes obtained with the thought of Mr. Gilbert White in mind. Mr. Gilbert White and his Timothy.

Eggs carefully re-packed in London, sea-shells too. Obviously fragile. But the tortoises are stowed in the empty boot of the Kensington coach.

Deeply inertial creatures, we tortoises are. Used to the steady gradations of our own locomotion. Mild acceleration. Step by step measure of uneven terrain. The rise and fall of a ship's progress is unpleasant. Still worse the way I was basketed to Ringmer, panniered beside a servant's hip. Earthed and boxed for the violent ride to Selborne by post-chaise.

But to be set—loose!—in a wooden coach-boot and driven south along the coach-road to Alton! Brisk and well in the morning after thousands of miles by sea. Then a purgatory of jolts and poundings! Over the dismal track to Selborne! Dashed again and again from top to bottom, side to side! A thunder of one's own! A hailstorm of self! Din of destruction, minute after minute, hour after hour, mile after mile!

Male tortoise mortally wounded. Who knows at what point in that fatal route. Jumbled to death. Killed by his own momentum. Churned out of life, though he did not finally perish until that night. Shell undamaged. But the fragility of the flesh within it demonstrated beyond a doubt. The very reason for that armor.

In the morning sun Mr. Charles Etty and Mr. Gilbert White place the female tortoise upon the grass-plot. Mrs. John White at their side, garden shears in hand. Thomas finds me among the poppies and sets me beside the stranger. As witness? Counselor? Token of benign intent?

Her gibbous dome rises as abruptly as the Hanger. As convex—as yellow—as the hunter's moon half-horizoned in early October. Finely checkered, tiled in alternate triangles the color of a ram's horn. Somberly toothed along the lower edges of her carapace. Bright bony plates discontinuously curved. Scutes sutured as if each were a more ingenious solution to the same problem. Head and neck and legs no less vivid—no less amber—than her shell. Sunlight embraces her and everyone around her.

"A very grand personage!" Mr. Gilbert White says, stooping in admiration.

"Very grand!" says the young sailor, who has seen her, far grander, where she naturally belongs.

I stand beside her. Nearly of a size, though her shell rises like a haystack above me. Not kin, not even kind. Yet near enough in nature to know that she is on the point of death. Pupils as dark as mine, as reflective, as pooling. I cannot say that she sees me. Already looking far within. A bright film comes over her eye. A fall of cobwebs against the sun. Legs arch and tense, and in the grass behind her she posits a single egg. Then dies. Sinking to rest on her tiled underbelly.

It is a curious moment. Shell still glistens in the frolicking sun. Dome swells as high as it did just then. Legs, propped up by the purchase she took on the turf, have not yet relaxed. Only her head and tail have fallen. Beak slightly open. Crusted like the shore of an algal pond.

Something, it seems, has passed from her to the egg. But the egg lies inanimate. The limbo of her breed. On that African island, far away, it might have hatched some months from now, if it had survived predations of the nest. Here it can only spoil. Misguided by the aberrations of this climate.

Mr. Gilbert White picks up the egg. Mr. Charles Etty gathers the tortoise. Mrs. John White walks toward the shrubbery on Baker's Hill. Thomas after her, to his stone garden roller. I am left to make my way back to the poppies, having seen what I could not help seeing.

Just another small corpse. Ten and a quarter pounds when weighed. What makes her different isn't her beauty or her scarcity or the distance she traveled in order to die here. It is this. The humans meant her to live.

Mr. Gilbert White, better than anyone, could guess what a probable surfeit of life lay before her. A more than human expanse of days. How that changes the calculation—how her death differs from that of the green woodpecker laughing at all the world but expecting to see only one more summer—Mr. Gilbert White is unable to say. Never having put the question to himself in so many words.

At his work-table, he clears the contents of her body. Any faint regret undone by the habit of the knife, the disassembly of such an interesting creature. Finds thirty eggs waiting. Cleans the carapace in the water-tub. Dries it carefully. Daubs the interior with one of his preserving concoctions and sets it on a shelf to dry. Then tea.

What will become of her shell? For a time it will stand for the whole tortoise—that lustrous being—in the memory of those who saw her living. In a Madagascar clearing. On a sunny Hampshire grass-plot in the month of July in the very last moments of her life. The shell will become, for Mr. Charles Etty at least, the memento of a grand youthful voyage. Utterly contrary to the quiet, unventuresome spirit of his father, Mr. Andrew Etty. Who used to say that he would not cross Selborne common at night for £50.

Then the shell becomes a curio, an uncommon object of unusual beauty or interest. Separate from the identity of the creature who grew it and wore it. Testimony to a type, not an individual. To something more general even than type. Perhaps it enters one of the grand apothecary shops that humans call museums. Exhibited to the curious at half a guinea a head.

More likely it merely takes on the dust of years. Demoted to a hallway table. The sort where Mrs. Rebecca Snooke's curiously hinged tortoise-shells lay. (And what became of *them* once the good old lady died?) One day, maid or grandchild brushes against it. Dashes it to the floor. The shell cracks, dried by time. Some earnest soul putties it together. And then—decades hence, an entirely separate longevity—it comes apart for good.

· · · · · ⌣

Undimmed glow of her carapace in the sunshine. Pallor of that egg. So long hidden, carried from Madagascar to this Hampshire garden. No knowing what brought it out of her at last. Whether it was ripe to be laid at any cost. Whether a clasping in her bowels drove it from her. Where she believed herself to be, if belief she had as she died.

But in dying her sex became manifest. Not by comparison to the male of the species. Not by form or color or size or by the parts of generation. Plain proof of the egg behind her in the grass. Testament round and white and "much resembling in size & shape the egg of an owl." Witnesses besides Mr. Gilbert White. A pure, if accidental, accession of knowledge. Evidence absolute, as rare as it is complete.

My own case is far less unequivocal. Nest-making devoted to personal hibernation. No eggs buried under the monk's rhubarb or hidden at the foot of the muscadine vine. None laid on the grass-plot. No preening, no dalliance. No seasons of the kind the mares enjoy, heat of the bitches, fervor of the gilts coming into their own. None of the endless, head-bobbing suggestions that ducks fling after drakes. Who would there be to fling mine upon?

And so Mr. Gilbert White has always *supposed* that I am male.

Perfectly able to sex a swallow, the curate is, even though

celibate. As alert to the sex of swallows as swallows them-
selves. At roost, on the wing, in the nest. Scouting over the
Hanger. Taking flies off the sides of the church-tower.
Skimming over a newly penned fallow.

But when he writes about swallows, Mr. Gilbert White
worries what sex to *say* they have. Despite the fact.

"I *had* used the pronoun personal feminine to my swallows," he tells his Gibraltar brother, now dead. "But some-
body objected, so I put *it* in its place; but I think you are
right, and shall replace *she* and *her*; though there is this
objection, that in a *pair* a male is implied, as well as a
female; and yet *he* would sound awkward for a bird."

Small wonder then that he has mistaken my sex. Perhaps
*she* would sound awkward for a tortoise. For the *Timothy* that
Mr. Henry Snooke bestowed upon me so long ago in
Chichester. A foolish assumption, a giving in to alliteration.
Perhaps Mr. Gilbert White is also misled by the extrava-
gance of my adventures. Perhaps a sympathetic assumption
of companionship between us.

*Timothy* I have been this half century and more. *Timothy* I
shall be forever after, thanks to Mr. Gilbert White's scribbling. And yet not wholly, never wholly, *Timothy*.

Mr. Gilbert White will clear the contents of my body if I
die first. (He will go as surely to his own grave intact.)
Sundered, shell drying on a shelf against the wall. But can
he read the arrangement of my internal organs? I am not
one of his birds or small mammals, whose innards he

knows like the parish horse-paths. He will not find the egg-road he finds inside the viper. No train of eggs, even the germs of eggs, waiting patiently to give my secret away.

None of the signs of the female. None that a curate would notice. Flare in the rounding of my carapace means nothing to him. But female I am and have always been since that moment in the egg decades ago. Female I was in that ancient country.

This climate, this England, has neutered me.

Winter of the human year 1740. My first at Mrs. Rebecca Snooke's. It came entirely unexpected. A stronger prompting to dig than I had ever known. Calling for a haste I did not have. Half-buried in that mired bed was as deep as I got. Half-numbed before half-buried. Mud congealing around me. Shell bare to the winds tumbling over the courtyard wall. Not the warm, dry northerlies of home. Damp howling fresh from the Arctic. Frost thrust deep into the ground. Soil heaved and buckled. Stone cast up onto the furrow. Tortoise onto the clod.

No rousing to find a warmer bed, a sounder roost. A deadly torpor instead. As though my blood had drained away and frozen beneath me. No rest in it. Sleep—if sleep it was—was a bare clinging to life. When I rose again at last, even the humans seemed dazed by what they had suffered. The hunger of spring—hungriest of seasons—seemed painfully welcome to them.

There have been winters more bitter by far. 1757. 1768.

1776. 1784. Country in tatters after each of them. Humans and sheep with the same raw look in their eyes, the survivors, well into March. But even in mild winters—mild for this England—I lie dormant far too long. Week after week, month after month. Vastly beyond the bounds set for my nature.

December in Selborne. My first. Summer-like weather, insects in air. Moss placed carefully over my back by Thomas where I lie. Light, mellow soil, well-drained. Warm border under the fruit-wall. Bees still at play before their hives. Meliorating influence of the Hanger. And yet out runs the tide of sleep, for months on end.

Even this past winter. Still stirring in December under a tuft of long grass. Flies droning overhead. Toadflax blooming. Hare nestled under a cabbage, waiting to nibble the pinks. Dry spell as the old year ends, barely a freeze at all in the new. Yet instead of a brief coasting voyage under fair skies, land in sight, balmy current, I plunge for the mid-ocean deeps. No turning back. No catching myself on the drift. Untoward plummet to the bottom.

Only the natural buoyancy of life itself carries me back to the surface, year after year. Mr. Gilbert White comes direct from the potato-bed to stare down at me with Thomas. Bees on the crocuses. Redstart in the high-wood. Song of the walk-mowing people. Unlimited sky overhead. Irrelevant remarks of a human towering high above me. Timotheus and his lyre once again. Singsong words. Like warm spring rain on my back. How welcome the confusion of voices in my ear!

To and fro of this climate. It has unsprung my vitals. Stalls me for months on end. Some internal weather has gone awry. Carried to the thin edge of life every winter. Everything at cross-purposes in my hybernaculum. Waves running out from shore, breaking far away in mid-ocean. Rain falling upward. Sun showing itself in phases like the moon. Crescent, gibbous, and the new sun, worst of all. Rising dark in a dark sky, just at the far corner of my winter's orbit, as I finally turn toward spring once more.

At last I return, alone, here to this garden. No longer a nest of unlaid eggs—a settlement—inside me. What year I came back empty I cannot say. But I am an abandoned city. Inhabitants stolen. Plagued. Driven off. Murdered. Gone up into the hills to perform some ancient rite. To bribe some failed fertility. Hecatombs and oil ineffective, if hecatombs and oil there were. Never to come back again. As if they forgot the pull of home once they left it. Call of those tombs. Ease of those baths. Lintels. Gods. Fresh water from a spring. Sea at their feet, pines at their shoulders.

That demise caused me no suffering. No particular sadness about the possibilities withered within me. I lost none of my maternity. In Cilicia, I would have laid those eggs in a scrape in the ground and wandered off. Duty accomplished. Generation served, as Mr. Gilbert White would say. Nothing further to be done. Any of those clutches prey to a raven or a weasel. Broken up, broken apart. The predator here is stealthier far. Fifteen degrees of northern latitude. All my eggs at once.

Had I laid them year by year in the Cilician scrub, I would never have known how many of my progeny lived. Now I do know. That is the difference. I feel merely the discordance of it all. One less hunger. The time of the male tortoise comes. No urge to seek him out. I lack the impulse as much as I lack the male himself. As though the swallows were to rise on the wing in September and, thinking better of it, settle back onto their roosts and winter here.

If the Great Mead were crowded with males of my kind, clamoring at the foot of the ha-ha—hissing at each other, necks outstretched—I would still miss the yearning. The superfluity I need to seek him out has been taken from me. Little by little. Every winter I have spent in this savage Atlantic weather. I no longer have wants to intimate, unlike the rest of the females in Selborne. Only enough life left for myself. Little enough of that.

The ewe requires the ram and makes it known. The bitch-fox, yipping, summons her mate. The famous Selborne sow, sagacious and artful, walks to a distant farm when the time is upon her. Opening gates as she goes, letting herself into the boar's pen. Several days conversing. Then she excuses herself and homeward again. So abhorrent is celibacy to the sex. Who knows what the village women say to their men? How does Nanny Hale urge her farmer a year or two after the wedding? What they may do in the night I cannot say.

· · · · · ⌒

**M**r. Gilbert White observes that a snake sloughs its skin like a stocking or a woman's glove. Turned wrong side outward. Intricately involves its length among the grasses in a mid-September field. Then unsheathes itself. The reptile changes its coat. The curate's homely metaphor.

"Thus it appears," he writes, "that snakes crawl out of the mouth of their own sloughs, & quit the tail part last; just as eels are skinned by a cookmaid."

Divine service at St. Mary's. Graveyard all about. Trunk of a mighty yew. Selborne street down the slope through the Plestor. Dorton down the other way. Toward Oakhanger stream and the lane beyond Peasecod's house.

"Abrupt, uneven country," Mr. Gilbert White calls his parish, "full of hills and woods, and therefore full of birds." Church of England. No papists, no Protestant dissenters. Therefore full of parishioners. Gathering on the mild mount where St. Mary's stands.

They all hope to change their coats in the grass of that graveyard. Throw their enamel'd skins, as the poet says. Rise new-sighted from death someday. So they say at morning and evening prayers, on feast days and Sundays. In earnest appeal to their god. All-perfect Donor. Article of faith strong among them. Awaiting the new raiment of new life. After being skinned by the cookmaid death.

From his seat in heaven, God the naturalist contemplates that difficult transition. Tender predicament of the new-sloughed Christian. So similar to the molting snake. Scales from its very eyes peel off in the molt, like spectacles. Mr. Gilbert White's words. "While the scales of the eyes are growing loose, & a new skin is forming, the creature, in appearance, must be blind, & feel itself in an awkward, uneasy situation."

The condition of their faith. Awkward, uneasy, blind. Hope and the fear of what lies beyond the grave. Fear uppermost all their lives.

In his study, Mr. Gilbert White examines the serpent's skin. A ghostliness about it. Reflection left in the mirror. Isinglass remnant. He peers through the discarded scales of the snake's eyes. Right side outward, as the reptile used them. Discovers that those lenses "lessen objects much."

When compounded by the lens of the human eye, that is. One animal gazing through the eye of another. The thought does not present itself in that form to Mr. Gilbert White. Who, like the rest of his breed, rarely considers himself an animal.

"It would be a most entertaining sight," he writes, "could a person be an eye-witness to such a feat, & see the snake in the act of changing his garment."

A better sight yet to see the change the parishioners and their curate pray for.

Naturalist in the field. Watching closely. Reasonable chance of observing a snake in its molt. Parting from itself. Extruding a new serpent. Reasonable chance of coming upon the snake's discarded skin and then, some distance off, the snake itself. Scales newly gilded, writhing away.

But there is no coming upon the new man, the new woman. No coming upon the shuck of these praying beasts. That old surrendered flesh. No catching them as they tran- substantiate. They bury all they have to leave behind. All they have to carry forward.

Wheat that was lodged rises again. Not the dead. Buried they remain. Turf thick over the coffins in St. Mary's ceme- tery. Graves still sealed on an Easter morning with a high rumbling wind. In the equinoctial blasts of autumn. In the amazing tempest of 1703, which felled the great oak in the Plestor. Stone steps around it. Seats above.

"The delight of old and young," the elders report. "A place of much resort in summer evenings; where the former sat in grave debate, while the latter frolicked and danced before them."

Mr. Gilbert White has buried them all in his life—old, young, former, latter, the grave and the frolicking. More than four hundred interred in his time. By the grave-side again and again. Reads the words—"With whom do live the spirits of them." Intones the prayers. Marks the grief. But can't help noticing how deep the January frost has entered the ground. Can't help thinking of Timothy under the walnut leaves. Soil bound by a foot of winter.

Is death so fearsome that it must be undone? Is this life so poor a thing? Is not eternity somewhat too long?

Theirs is a niggardly faith, withal. Parishioners believe only as much as will save the humans among them. Never mind the rest of creation. Unwilling to distinguish the dead from the living. But eager to set apart the rest of creation.

Eleventh Sunday after Trinity. Mid-August. Michaelmas daisies in bloom. Sun, shower, gleam, clouds. Sixty-three degrees. Suppressed air of festival. St. Mary's is hung with faded garlands in honor of village girls reputed to have died virgins. White paper gloves and knots and roses. "Reputed" is Mr. Gilbert White's word. Man of evidence as well as faith.

He rises to the pulpit. God's family, he says, is numberless. "Comprehending the whole race of mankind." And only the race of mankind. Thereby cutting off most of creation.

But numberless is not the race of mankind. Numberless is the race of beetles. Numberless are "the most insignificant insects and reptiles." Flying ants that swarm by millions in this garden. Armies of aphids falling in showers over the village. Palmer-worms hanging by threads from the oaks. Shoals of shell-snails. The earthworms. Mighty, Mr. Gilbert White avers, in their effect on the economy of nature. Yet excluded from the family of god.

Humans believe that the parish of Earth exists solely for

their use. Fabric of cottages, roofs, sheds, and shops. Shelter of brew-houses, malt-houses, ash-houses, granaries, kilns. Hand-work in brick and wood. Slate, stone, thatch. Greensand, blue rag, wattle. Walks and alleys and side-yards through this village. The comfort of the human establishment. Chambers and hearths as welcoming as a human face. Houses looking out on street and Hanger with great staring human eyes.

But martins brood among the eaves in the street as if the eaves had been hung for them. Coal-mice in the overhang of a thatched house as if thatched for them. Daws in the oaken church-shingles as though shingled for no other purpose. Owls hiss and screech like goblins in the tower, high above the churchyard. Their right to the tower as absolute as the vicar's. They flutter at the windows of the dying. Alarming the weak-minded, the more than usually superstitious. Swallows dash up and down the village street and over the garden walks. Redbreasts fly into houses and soil the furniture with elderberry droppings.

Crickets ring on the moist kitchen-hearth, singing against rain. Harvest-bugs bite the ladies in ways and places their spouses never do. Fleas and mites lodge in the skin and hair and feathers of every creature, no matter how reasonable. Flies in the dining room. Bats under the chimney-leads as morning rises. A living to be eked out in every corner, no matter how tiny. Shelter in every crevice. Village alive with the creation, humans vastly outnumbered.

# Timothy

Nearly seven hundred humans in the parish. Many thousands of Blattae swarming in just one of the neighboring houses. Males through the casements of open windows on a hot summer night.

Yet from the pulpit humans and animals form separate parishes. One in spiritual communion with the creator. The other—herds and flocks and swarms and tribes and troops—the parish of the merely created. The louse under the shirt of a Sunday parishioner leaves St. Mary's unblessed. No matter how its host prays. Eyes screwed shut. Hands folded. Beseeching hard. A next life, please, with no biting and sucking insects.

⌇ • • • • •

**M**r. Gilbert White in the pulpit to the worshipful of Selborne.

God, he says, has set up a light "in the breast of every partaker of Human Nature." A common badge called reason. Faculty distinguishing man from beasts.

"The principle of all Knowledge," he calls it. The very how of going about knowing his god.

More custom than reason in the liturgy. More hope than knowledge. No surfeit of reason in Selborne either. Custom a vastly stronger force in the village. Habit of their lives. Smoother path. Doing as their fathers and mothers did. Believing as they believed. Building as they built. Seeing exactly what they expect to see and very little else. Reverting to fear when they don't. Superstition sucked in with mothers' milk. Tide of a credulous faith always on the flood.

Set loose in this garden I stride down the long walk. Spring 1780. Back and forth along the ha-ha, that mere brick breastwork. My discernment puzzles Mr. Gilbert White. He notes with surprise what he calls my powers of instinct.

Timothy the tortoise, he writes, "is much too wise to walk into a well, for when he arrives at the haha, he distinguishes the fall of the ground, & retires with caution or marches carefully along the edge."

Mr. Gilbert White knows nothing of my ancient city. Its cisterns and baths. Rubble walls and necropolis. Cannot imagine me on a cornice overlooking the sea. Dozing on a sun-baked precipice. I know something of steep places. Something of the drop. The fall of the ground is plain to see.

Even Mr. John Ray—the naturalist's great antecedent— discovers more than bare instinct in the land-tortoise. Behavior that argues something of Reason in the reptile. He notes that a tortoise struggles to right itself, when over-turned, by using the lay of the land.

"Their Industry upon this Account," says the sagacious author, "is very admirable." Wisdom of god in the works of creation, if you like. Place a human at risk of death. Admire his industry in trying to escape it. Call it what you will— reason, instinct, superstition, faith.

# Timothy

But does Rover tumble off the edge of the ha-ha? Does Gunnory, the old bantam hen?

The force of instinct provokes Mr. Gilbert White. Purity of intention in the animal kind. Confidence of behavior. Diversity of birds' nests. Beauty of their design. Preciseness of their situations. He admires the sagacity of the willow-wren, who hides her brood with moss. Nest-ball of the harvest-mouse. Cradle suspended in the head of a thistle. Elegant instance of the efforts of instinct. The urge among cattle to stand in ponds when summer overheats. Belly-deep, mid-leg, as nature guides them.

"An undistinguishing, limited faculty," Mr. Gilbert White calls instinct. Sometimes above reason, he argues. Other times far below it. "That secret influence by which every species is impelled naturally to pursue, at all times, the same way or track, without any teaching or example."

Thus confining the brute creation to the cart-ways of love and hunger.

He chaffs Mr. Ralph Churton for his vagaries. His uncertainty planning the Christmas visit to Selborne.

"Pray come on the 24th," Mr. Gilbert White instructs, "for if you cannot be as regular in your migrations as a ring-ousel or a swallow, what is the use of all your *knowledge*? since it may be outdone by *instinct*."

Wheat harvest in the fields around the village. Binding in small sheaves. Ricking and gleaning. Bulls begin their shrill autumnal note. August the silent month for birdsong, except for the goldfinch.

Mr. Gilbert White to his parishioners.

Reason, he says, resembles a celestial flame. It "sparkles, and shines, and spreads out its luster every way; and extends itself to all parts of the Universe; and attracts to it not only present, but also past, and future objects, those in Heaven above, and in the earth beneath, and even under it."

Yet reason lacks certainty here in the thicket of ordinary life. None of the immediacy of instinct. Incontrovertible urging a martin feels in building her nest. Unfailing return of the swifts. Reason may sparkle and shine to all parts of the Universe, but it is a guttering candle to humans here in the dark. Light of a glow-worm when smoke lies low over the fields. Humans choose against reason—and the better reason of instinct—every day.

Caught in their "Will I?" "Shall I?" Which leg to put forth first.

Tottering, stilt-gaited beasts. A sad plight. Reason too often a will-o'-the-wisp. Instinct a relic within them.

The naturalist learns in time to seek wisdom wherever wisdom can be found. In the fern-owl. In the great bat of evening. In every species. Conviction growing upon Mr. Gilbert White as he ages. Sense of wonder rising within him. Not at the beauty of nature alone. But at what it knows.

Short-winged summer birds. Delicate beings. How, he wonders, do they "bear up against such storms of snow & rain, & make their way thro' such meteorous turbulencies, as one should suppose would embarrass & retard the most hardy & resolute of the winged nation? Yet they keep their appointed times & seasons, & in spite of frosts & winds return to their stations periodically as if they had met with nothing to obstruct them."

Can a bird be called foolish, he asks, "which knows the times and the seasons, and conducts its migrations over seas and continents with such accuracy and success?"

Can it be called foolish when it "is ready to repel intruders, and by menaces to defend to the best of its power its callow and helpless young!"

Mr. Gilbert White could preach a sermon upon the constancy of the swift. Unvarying cycle of its year. Eight or nine pair arrive in Selborne at the end of April. Retreat from it punctually by mid-August. Eleventh Sunday after Trinity. As true to their time as the solstice or the arrival of Findon, the Faringdon carrier.

They build under low thatched roofs along the street. Dash and frolic through Selborne. Around St. Mary's, above the glebe-close, and back again. Pursuing church-owls and hawks. Squeaking on wing until a quarter before nine in midsummer.

Dear to Mr. Gilbert White above all other birds, the swifts, though defective in architecture. Fledgling falls from the nest into the churchyard. Curate feeds it with flies. Tosses it back up onto the shingles. He studies the swifts with great penetration. Observes their behavior in every weather. How they mate in air. How their wings meet over their backs when they do so. How in Selborne they build under the "lowest and meanest cottages" as well as on the tower of St. Mary's. Theirs is an earthly ascension. Making no distinction between rich and poor.

Mr. Gilbert White instructs his nieces and nephews in the swift-like virtues. Punctuality, mildness, parental and spousal domesticity. Also their delight in existence. He is possessed by their wonderful powers of wing. Habit of feeding in the highest precincts of sky. The way thunderous weather stirs them.

Mr. Gilbert White stands in the melon-ground on Baker's Hill. Hat removed. Head thrown back. Hearing little enough now. Eyesight dimming. But gazing at swifts almost out of sight in the skies above the Ewel-close for half an hour on end. They live, he says, "more in the air than any other bird." They perform "all functions there save those of sleeping and incubation."

Are there to be no swifts in the skies of Mr. Gilbert White's heaven? No house-martins building under the thatched eaves of that celestial city? No tortoises in the gardens there? And what if instinct—so little known to humans, but a pure flame in swifts—is a surer guide than reason to his god?

And what if this earth is that heaven? No god in residence. No god needed. Every instant of this one life the god in itself.

Mr. Gilbert White could turn a sermon upon the swifts.

But he keeps his divinity and his natural history apart. Separate parishes after all.

The sermon he does make—a brief one—is upon the loon, the great northern diver. Rare visitor to Hampshire. Found alive on the heath. Alive at the time. Three drams short of three pounds. Wingspan forty-two inches. Rancid, inedible flesh.

But "so incomparably adapted to its mode of life," writes Mr. Gilbert White, that "in no instance do we see the wisdom of God in the Creation to more advantage."

Head proportioned to pierce the waves. Foot for swimming and diving. Wings mounted forward to propel the bird underwater. And yet the loon is excluded from the greater hope of humans. Attests to the wisdom of God in the Creation. But not a member of his family. Only a marker. A lump of bright chalk showing the way across Selborne common—the sheep-walk—in the dark of night.

· · · · · ⌢

**O**ne earthly parish—this only life.

"Nature is such an œconomist," Mr. Gilbert White writes, "that the most incongruous animals can avail themselves of each other!" Wagtails, he means, picking flies from the legs of cattle grazing in moist low pastures.

But are wagtails and cattle more incongruous than the cow and the girl who milks her? Than the cow and the girl and the harvest-bug that bites her? Intermingled all together in the economy of Nature.

Humans repose in the distinctness of their being. Family of god. Upright stature. Bipedal stride. Pride of reason. Pompion head. They hold themselves apart from the works of the creation as much as they can. Except for sporting and poaching. Breeding and rearing of barnyard animals. Coaxing wheat and barley and turnips out of the ground.

Nothing quite real until they see its reflection. They mirror the out-of-doors in their minds. Hold it up to the glass as a way of holding it apart. Framing it. Giving it perspective. Keeping the world at a murmurous rook-distance.

"The hanging beech-woods," Mr. Gilbert White writes, "begin to be beautifully tinged, & to afford most lovely scapes, very engaging to the eye, & imagination. They afford sweet lights & shades. Maples are also finely tinged. These scenes are worthy the pencil of a Rubens."

Every accoutrement divides them, in their own minds, from the kingdom of other creatures. Every practice, every artifice. Pencil of Rubens. Use of Florence-oil. Pepper. Spinning of wool. Art of tea. Shaving. Pounds and shillings and pence. Bills of exchange. News from abroad. London. Hymns of the prayerful. Songs of the drunk and bawdy. Tompion clock. Guinea subscription for the sick and lame in the county hospital. Silver spurs. Pinchbeck seal.

Separate in the curious act of reading. Eyes fixed to the page like a stoat staring down a field-mouse. Attention averted from everything else. Nosing along the trail of words. Mr. Ralph Churton strides across the grass-plot. Sheep bells. Calf bawling. Rill of birdsong. Deaf to it all. Duodecimo held head-high. Again through judicious Virgil, that notorious poacher from the Greek. Mumbling in time to something other than his footsteps. How does *he* avoid the ha-ha?

Dressing and undressing. Every garment a divorce from nature. Fine wove buttons. Silktwist stays. Fustian breeches. French camlet coat. Gloved and swaddled against the weather. Booted against mud. Chafing of stirrup-leather and horse-hide.

Wholly naked as little as possible. Shift off, shirt on as quickly as can be. Don't let the mirror see. Don't look down. Separate even from themselves. Hiding from the sallow under-belly. Organs of generation. Disdaining the flesh that keeps them from heaven.

Vocalizing in pairs and groups, like rooks. Not in solitude, like the redbreast or the titlark. No singing from wood to wood in sexual fervor. No bellowing in heat from field to field. Face to face instead along Selborne street. Nose to nose. Hand to hand. Arm in arm. Curious soft monotone of the human tongue. Nasal humming. The dried sticks and leaves of consonants. Whole ricks and granaries of meaning threshed each day.

*Lords* of the *Creation*. To all appearances set apart by reason, domicile, dress, and language. Best argument of god's intent they call themselves. Adducing, in evidence, the perfection of their size. Not too Pygmean to fight off a raven. Not too gigantic to ride a horse. Properly proportioned to manage the inferior creatures. So goes their curious, their infantile logic.

"So excellent a Piece of Workmanship," writes the Physico-Theologist of his own kind. "Such a Microcosm, such an Abridgement of the Creator's Art in him, as is alone sufficient to demonstrate the Being and Attributes of GOD."

No mention of a few unwelcome facts. Lack of a hard rind or a soft pelt. Cruelly exposed to frost and heat and hunger. Nothing ready at hand in this world for their use. No proper food. Always another tool to be fashioned. Another loaf to be baked. Another store-house to be built. No putting their heads down and grazing in May.

But able to argue upward from themselves to GOD. To discover in all that surrounds them—and especially in themselves—the manifestation of a great Creator. If only to admire what Mr. Gilbert White calls "the harmony and beauty of the works of the creation."

And to tell sentimental stories about it. Rook-murmur in the distance at the close of day. One of the curate's nieces listens for a moment. "Now the rooks are saying their prayers," she exclaims. A remark, Mr. Gilbert White adds, "in the true spirit of *physico-theology.*" An adorable falsehood.

The genuine story? Rooks look down upon St. Mary's from the Hanger on a Sunday morning. Stream of parishioners into the church. Stroke of the bells in the tower. Murmur of human voices from a distance, coming across the Ewell. Then silence. "Now the humans are saying their prayers," a rook observes, with absolute probity.

Some years chafers fall upon the village after wintering as rook-worms in the earth. Apple blossom and oak leaf come out in May. Hordes of rapacious beetles descend. Annoy the night air with their buzzing flight. Blunder into the cavities of my carapace. Rattle against candle-lit windows. Wherever they swarm the country stinks of them.

Chafers fall onto sheep from branches and leaves. Maggots ensue in the wool. Whole woods of oaks are eaten bare. Hedges and gardens defaced. Herb and leaf stripped. Field boys cannot drive the beetles off. Undeterred by farmers and gardeners and weeding women. Dogs of no avail. Cats flee. Hanger, field, and garden, thick with insects. Eating their fill. Devouring the downs. Naked leafless state of the world.

Chafer years: 1774, 1778, 1782, 1786. Everything would be destroyed.

But rooks in the thousands bring out their young and take the insects in flight. Daws from the church-tower come to Mr. Gilbert White's orchard, as if to acknowledge his curacy. Turkeys and house-sparrows work the grass-plots. Battening on the hordes. Feasting on the chafer-plague. Every fourth year it is good to be a rook. And when chafers fail, rooks live hard.

The beetle-storm passes. Oaks recover. Lammas-growth of beautiful foliage later in summer. But not the horse-chestnut. Beech and maple bare for the season. A predictable scourge.

In chafer years humans do not seem so separate from the rest of creation. When without rooks and daws they would famish.

Nor when rains fail and farmers plant in absolute dust. When wells dry up in the village. Mr. Gilbert White lengthens the well-rope and still brings up water foul and turbid. Unfit for brewing or washing. The spring at Kimber's mead fails. Pond on the common empties. In Newton great pond, only a few puddles remain for the villagers.

Grass burnt to a powder. Upland villages in distress. Mills at Hawkley and Greatham barely able to grind. Not enough water to turn the wheel. Barley for autumn hogs goes unmilled. Butter at ninepence a pound. Butter-pots go empty. Men watch the storm divide. Palpable hunger in their faces. Skirts of the southern tempest coast past Selborne without a drop.

Or is it worse when the rains persist? Wells overflow. Lavant through Cobb's courtyard. Country all in a flood. Hay rots on the ground. Rafts of it swept down-river from the meadows. Post-boys drowned. Gentlemen swimming from their chaises. Fields drenched and all the spring corn still abroad. Wheat rising in price. Very little left in the kingdom. Earth glutted. Fifty inches in a single twelvemonth, the human year 1782. Clover spoiled. Fodder in short supply. No forest-peat laid up for the poor. Even I nearly flood under the laurel hedge that March, till rescued by Thomas.

And always the dread of winter. Fear of the dark, the cold, the hunger. Day but a few hours of dim light. Scouring winds. Pitiful fires. Not nearly warm-blooded enough, these humans. Rover buries his nose under his tail. Finds a corner out of the draft. Poultry sink their heads in their down. Humans numb to the bone all winter long. Their heaven is only warm feet.

A sudden frost enters the house. Fresh provisions ruined. Bread, apples, potatoes, cheese. Boys slide on lakes merely to stay warm. Better than huddling, hungry, in the dark. Measles and colds and whooping cough drag down the villagers, already weakened. A hard winter destroys infants and the elderly. Kills blackbirds and larks and the poor, living on the gleanings of the farmers' fields. Better to be a hog carrying straw in January than a pauper.

But agriculture, Mr. Gilbert White writes, is now arrived at a pitch of perfection. Famines rare. Gardens improve. Gardeners get fortunes. Green-stalls in cities support multitudes. No one need eat salted flesh who has money to buy fresh. And what about those who can buy neither? This profusion is only two droughts and a bad winter deep. A feverish June cold makes its way from Russia. Bills of mortality swell. Up on their stilts of reason these humans catch every draft, every catarrh. Incessant labor merely to feed themselves. While I neither toil nor spin.

Mr. Gilbert White calls me a poor being, lost in torpor. Poor embarrassed reptile. But what have I not survived? Winter after winter, drought, and flood. No human devices or artifices. No fires or coal-scuttles. No need to dig wells or lay up provisions or cut and cock and thatch the sainfoin in order to feed the cattle that will fill the larder once butchered and hung in the pendant meat-safe. I feast in the seasonal variety of this garden. But I would dine just as well in the underbrush on the Hanger.

So strict an economist is nature. For humans no less. Hedged in by rainfall and frost, drying winds. Condemned to watch ricks swell and shrink. Prices rise and fall. Wells dry up and overflow. Sheep lamb and die. Nothing to do but make a larger pile of turnips. A more extensive flock. To lay by as much as possible against the uncertainty of the coming months.

"Since we must not expect plenty," Mr. Gilbert White writes, "till Providence sends us more favourable seasons."

Farmers stack wheat-sheaves in barn-mows. Thresh from the outside in. After a cold, damp harvest, the cold, damp flour comes first. The best wheat lies at the bottom of the mow, the miller says, and won't come forth till spring. So they earnestly hope. Reason is the parlor-fire that warms their toes. Hope is the heath-fire, burning whole hillsides, making a great smoke among them.

## Timothy

"Cold-blooded" is the story that humans tell of reptiles. But we thrive, humans and reptiles, on the same heat. From the same source. They draw theirs indirectly. I draw mine direct. Lie under the fruit-wall in the warmth of the winter sun. Shell tilted to catch those feeble rays. Absorb the planet's heat from deep underground. Hunger set aside for half the year.

A human lying under the fruit-wall is at best a vagabond. Won't lie there for long. Hunger gets him up—if Thomas, with a digging prong, doesn't stir him first. Culprit who robs Mr. Gilbert White's apricot tree. One of the poor who steal farmers' corn in the night after a bitter winter. A human lying in the winter sun, as I do, is likely a corpse.

Enterprise, Mr. Gilbert White calls this human fever. Warm-blooded inability to leave off eating. Incessant calls for replenishment. Always another round to be paid for, somehow. Dinner a worry before breakfast digested. Whole of creation down the maw of man. Merely to keep the kiln warm. A cruel slavery it is. All while the earth reeks with heat.

• • • • • ⌒

I rose early that day.

Soon after cock-crow. Fully awake for the first time in months. Hunger everywhere I look. Scent of the Provence rose famishes me. Cucumbers bristling inside their dripping hand-glasses. Blossoms still clinging to succulent fruit. I graze in the grass-walk till the sun begins to lift the dew. Shadows still wet. Skeins of spider-web across the fields.

I stride down the garden on the points of my claws. A bustle in my blood. Long of leg. Pertinacious tail. Exceptionally brisk. Strikingly mobile. As animated as the pettichaps in the crown-imperials.

Walking elate, Mr. Gilbert White calls it, when a May morning strikes me this way. My earnestness he takes as a sign of impending rain. At the first drop, he supposes, I shall run my head up in a corner. As if I were "a lady dressed in all her best attire, shuffling away on the first sprinklings." I scarcely know the timid reptile of whom he writes. I who slept on Byzantine walls. Who clawed Mediterranean sands. Climbed the Tarsus. Crossed the seas to England.

Wicket-gate stands open. No one by. What is there to deter me? No surtout to pack. No mare to saddle. No instructions to Mrs. John White. No guineas or bank-notes to tuck into my tiled waistcoat. Out I go.

Leaving only questions behind me.

"How?" The wicket-gate.

"Where?" The bean-field just short of the Pound Field.

"Why?" Above all, why?

Why is two questions. How could I leave such a paradise? After everything we gave you. Needs provided for. Immoderate safety. Kindness, even affection of its humans. Voice of the naturalist in the cool of the day. Refuge from the sun under the shade of my dinner.

But also: what impels me? What spurs me on? What is my motive in venturing forth? Mr. Gilbert White imagines only one.

Thomas catches me up in his hands. Returns me to the asparagus in the din of Daniel Wheeler's boy. Calm comes over the garden. Mrs. John White returns to the kitchen. Goody Hammond to her singing and blossom-sweeping. Thomas goes back to the barn. That evening Mr. Gilbert White takes up the pen to Miss Molly White. To summarize *why*.

Timothy, he writes, "had conceived a notion of much satisfaction to be found in the range of the meadow, and Baker's Hill; and that beautiful females might inhabit those vast spaces, which appeared boundless in his eye. But having wandered 'til he was tired, and having met with nothing but weeds, and coarse grass, and solitude, he was glad to return to the poppies, and lettuces, and the other luxuries of the garden."

H*e*, indeed.

The fable that humans love to tell. One bright morning the prodigal tortoise sallies forth. Rich in notions. Wealthy in prospect. But the world is an unrelenting place. Lonely. Coarse grass. Weeds. Imaginary females. Alas the comforts of home. Luxuries of the garden. Old settled ways. Rejoicing over the lost sheep. Fatted calf. A mammals' tale told to the sound of a crackling fire. Never leave home unsure of your next good blaze.

Mr. Gilbert White offers another version in that book of his. "The motives that impel him to undertake these rambles," he notes, "seem to be of the amorous kind: his fancy then becomes intent on sexual attachments, which transport him beyond his usual gravity, and induce him to forget for a time his ordinary solemn deportment."

The organ of fancy, where is it lodged? How does it come to be so vacant in tortoises? Empty of all but the thought of sexual attachments.

No human thinks more liberally of the brute creation than Mr. Gilbert White. His every day devoted to their study. Glimpsing the inwardness of their lives. Coherence of their conversation. Domesticated or wild. In hedge, hanger, or stream. On wing, foot, fin, or belly. As well-versed in the ring ousel and goatsucker as he is in the farmer and maid.

Larks in January. Vast congregations. Snow, dark and still. Mr. Gilbert White cannot account for their flocking in winter. Not a time for mating. Food scarce. What draws the birds together? Perhaps larks flock together, Mr. Gilbert White suggests, out of helplessness in rigorous seasons. "As men crowd together, when under great calamities, though they know not why."

Common wellspring, shared alike among animals and humans. Only an analogy, but a tender one. Also a confession of sorts. Sometimes humans do things *they know not why*.

## Timothy

Severe tempest. Body torn by the storm from the gibbet on Hind-head. Damage to shipping in Portsmouth. Rigging in tatters. Men crowd the docks to see the battered hulls. *They know not why.*

Opera house in the Haymarket burns. Men watch the embers as if roasting potatoes among them. Crowding together to share the burden of this judgment. Comfort in the presence of their fellows. Even the pickpockets are somehow consoling. Cries of the ballad-sellers. *They know not why.*

Humans have their motives. As many as they care to name. Reason is a warehouse full of motives. But only two—says the naturalist—can belong to the viper and the owl. Only love and hunger to drive the swifts and martins and all the beasts of Selborne. The urge "to perpetuate their kind." And "to preserve individuals."

The action of every animal, every insect comes down at last to this overwhelming purpose: "the intercourse between the sexes."

True enough perhaps. But mark the application. Judge the naturalist as narrowly as he judges the rest of creation. Merely a beast like any other, after all. Tottering, stilt-gaited, praying, reasoning. Man of system. Man of the cloth. But blood, brain, bowels, and bile nonetheless.

Every day carries the curate somewhere. Over the Hanger toward Newton. Along Combwood to Oakhanger or Priory Farm. To Alton or Faringdon or Emshot. To St. Mary's or the vicarage at the very least. By post-chaise. On horseback. On foot. Alone and in company.

His motive?

It cannot be hunger. Mr. Gilbert White is a lean eater. Mrs. John White looks after the provisions of his house. Garden crowded with vegetables, early and late. Coss and Dutch lettuces stand winter-long under the fruit-wall, sheltered beneath straw. Bantams lay all summer. Cellar full. Port wine bottled in Selborne from the hogshead. Cider, French brandy, raisin wine. Strong-beer brewed in the Wilts method, fine as rock-water. Sugar loaves on a kitchen shelf. Meat-pantry buzzing in the walnut tree, well-provisioned with a joint of beef.

Mr. John Hale over the way commands for the asking a ready supply of mutton and veal. London wagon comes as near as Faringdon. Hams and baskets of oysters and good Iceland codfishes. If Mr. Gilbert White merely troubles his niece to send them. Bushels of apples and pears from the garden. Preserves of every kind. In January he tubs and salts up a fine young hog raised by Timothy Turner. Nine-score pounds of pork.

If not hunger, then his motive must be love. Amorous dalliance. Serving his generation as well as his Captain. Succoring widows. Anointing wives. Catechizing daughters. Carrying the seed as well as the gospel. Spreading a clerical honeydew over the parish.

To what other motive can the naturalist attribute such

roamings? Why else does the curate take so much trouble? The very question he might ask of the linnet or stag.

Folly to think so, of course. The curate has more than the two strings of love and hunger to tug at. A larger, more complicated *why* in humans, he believes, than gorging and rutting.

And so why not in the rest of creation?

*How*, the naturalist begins to understand, after years of study. He records the *when* and *where* and *which* of the birds of passage, beasts of the field. Those are the very questions that system is poised to answer. But *why* will never be solved by system. No number of small corpses, dissected, tagged, and preserved, will ever begin to answer *why*.

How the nightingale sings. Pitch of the notes. Melody of the song. Structure of the voice box. But never fully the nightingale's *why*.

"Woodmen tell me," Mr. Gilbert White notes, "that fernowls love to sit upon the logs of an evening: but what their motive is does not appear."

Is not the love of sitting upon logs of an evening motive enough? What is the motive for taking tea at the Hermitage on a blue afternoon, gray and still? To understand the motives of the rest of creation Mr. Gilbert White will have to consult his own.

But humans are blinded—even the naturalist—by being human. Barely able to witness what is not human. Always conjuring with the separateness of their species. Separate creation. Special dominion. Embarrassed by signs of their animal nature. Veritable teats. Undeniable pizzle. Thank GOD for reason. Distant relations at best, the birds and beasts of the parish. Cut out of the will. Scratched out of the family Bible.

Mr. Gilbert White rides over the common from Newton. Late May in the human year 1784. Reins his Galloway mare at the crest of the Hanger. Every manner of living thing in sight or in memory on this sweet, warm evening.

Bees thriving. Flycatcher nesting under the parlor window. Kestrel hovering over the hay-field below. Ravens tumbling in flight. Swifts nearly lost in the clouds. Rooks at their endless beech-top quarrels. Swallows taking food up and down the river. Feeding their young in exact rotation. Mare beneath him feeling the pull of home. Tortoise making her escape into the fields among the grass.

"Brute beasts that have no understanding," says the prayer-book. Driven only by love and hunger. Driven *they know not why*.

~ • • • • •

**B**ut I know why. Forty-four years among humans by the time I escaped through the wicket-gate. Nine years more down to this present day. I am not natured for it. Not fitted for their proximity.

Fine beings in a way. Well-adapted to their own presence. Inventive to a fault. Resourceful. What is there in this world, asks the physico-theologist, "that man's contrivance doth not extend unto, and make some way or other advantageous to himself?"

But they belong in the far distance. Rare glimpses. Drab, thin figures moving against the backdrop of the sea. Across a clearing near that ancient odeon. Set upon their own poor passage through the country. Stopping to sleep. Fill a goat's-bladder at a freshwater spring. Tend a cook-fire in the shade of a cistern. No time to take interest in a tortoise musing on a rubble wall. Minding their business. Moving on. Taking their contrivance with them.

And I am as captive now as the day I was shoved in a bag and stowed in a ship's belly. Mr. Gilbert White thinks only to ask what I'm escaping toward. Not what I'm escaping from. But then he is the gardener. His is the garden. Runnel of his life has washed down the same course all these years. He lives in the place of his birth. To imagine escape he must imagine enticement.

Not quite the old interrogatory in that look of his, the one from Ringmer days and early Selborne. Then, I was a mere quantum of tortoise to him. Experimental substance to be tried against certain hypotheses. But Mr. Gilbert White ages. Even less of the little flesh on his cheeks. A something of Mrs. Rebecca Snooke in the lines on his face. Nervous cough. Gout reddens his left hand, shooting and burning. Now it wanders to other extremities. His gravel comes and goes. Feverish disorder with it.

And yet he sows kidney-beans in the ground, iron-hard after a long dry spring. Cuts cucumbers as they ripen and offers me the parings. Waters the poplar at the foot of the Bostal. Measures the largest beech in Sparrow's hanger—object of special veneration—with his brother, Mr. Benjamin White. Keeps the weather daily as he has done these forty years.

He has christened the parish, married the parish, buried the parish. Served this village nearly all his days. Forsaken other chances for it. Other lives. His look at last suggests that we are both caught up in the same hypothesis. The same experiment. For a natural historian, it is a great step forward.

Mr. Gilbert White's kindness toward me has not abated. Flawed only by the fact of my captivity. His inability to restore me to my birthright. To a place he knows nothing of. I am not some fledgling swift to be stuffed with flies and tossed back up onto the church-shingles.

Among the humans, some are gamekeepers, some shepherds. Some are good at coppice-work. Others prefer the long furrow and the company of a plow-horse. Some are mowers whose scythes set the pace. The maltster differs in outlook and habits from the miller. Butcher and blacksmith are as different as whole lives in their livelihoods can make them. They know little of the shopkeeper's turn of mind or the surveyor's. Brickburner understands the mason's job but cannot lay a plumb wall himself. Sawyer cannot fill in professionally for saddlemaker or hedge-layer. Nor can any of these men mend a shirt or embroider a bride's linen or keep a house as trim as a ship of the line, the way the women of Selborne can.

Not a human in the parish who can do for himself everything needed to live. Unless he lives as meagerly and cannily as a fox. To each man and woman a vocation of one kind or another, no matter how humble. All fitted together in the economy of Selborne.

Even the curate. Reading aloud on Sundays. Directing the bowing of heads and the closing of eyes. Parting living and dead. Joining man and woman. Sprinkling infants. Visiting the sick. Cheering the downhearted. Overseeing the small charities vested in him. A matter of £10 annually to teach poor parish children how to write, sew, knit, and say their prayers. To bind them out as apprentices and servants. Merely to be human is not nearly enough.

But what is the heron's vocation? To what occupation is the viper called? Or summer's myriad of frogs? What trade was the otter following when he strayed down the rivulet?

Only a single vocation in all the rest of this earthly parish, all the rest of creation. Vocation of place.

Fern-owl feeds aloft with cunning claw. Osprey plunges to gather its food. Thrush eats shell-snails. Bullfinch, honeysuckle buds. Martin, *coleoptera*. No matter how they get their living, they get their living where they must. Ages of ancestors fit them for marsh or hedge or underwood beech. Expert in their terrain. Minutely particular in habitation. Fitted just so into the mosaic of Selborne. Some to dwell here all their lives. Some, like the ring ousel, merely to use the parish hills "as an inn or baiting place." One occupant only to live forever displaced.

Stone-curlew never strides through the garden poppies. Never makes her evening flight at noon. Nowhere but where she is fitted to. Among the gray-spotted flints that match her feathering. Clamoring in upland fields and sheep-walks. Who she is, a matter of where she is. The path she takes in migrating, long legs strung out behind her. The place she comes to rest.

Rook in the beech-tops. Trout in the stream. Owl in the high-wood. Cricket in the damp. Wild pigeons "reaching in strings for a mile together as they went out in a morning to feed." Before Magdalen College cut its wood on the Hanger. Place is what they practice, an all-sufficient knowledge.

Some live narrowly. Insects moored in the county of a single oak-crown. Like the milkmaid who has never left her corner of the parish.

Others live in place more extensively than Mr. Gilbert White can imagine. As widely as Mr. Charles Etty, who voyages nearly round the world. Surviving shipwreck, stranding, the groaning and leaking of crazed vessels.

# Timothy

Stationary voyagers, some of them. Barnacles encrusting the hull. Shipworm infesting it. As fixed in place—beating across mid-ocean—as the tern overhead in her age-old route under the stars.

All summer long the short-winged soft-billed birds flit from hedge to hedge. Ambit of only a few dozen yards. Yet when that other-life-place pulls in autumn, they go to unimaginable trouble. Unimaginable to the naturalist.

"That such feeble bad fliers," Mr. Gilbert White exclaims, "should be able to traverse vast seas and continents in order to enjoy milder seasons amidst the regions of Africa!" As inexplicable to him as the longevity of a tortoise.

"I am at a loss even what to suspect about them," he writes.

But those birds are students of their profit as surely as the governors of the East India Company. Routes more fixed, more certain than the Company's ships. Sense of place firmly bound to their sense of time. Wheeling about the year, across the globe. Following their vocation.

・ ・ ・ ・ ◠

**M**r. Gilbert White mocks his own fixedness. Rooted in Selborne. Calls himself "a venerable vegetable, remaining like a cabbage on the same spot for months together." But if a cabbage were human, it would aspire to become a lettuce. Pull up roots and go up to town to see what's doing in the artichoke way. Such a restless tribe. Such a turbulent animal, as Mr. Gilbert White says of the hog.

No proper *where* to these humans. Any*where* will do. The only indispensable *where* for them is among other humans. Smell of cottage smoke through the trees. October mist over the rich corn-vales. Dividing a lottery ticket among themselves, the little farmers, servants, and laborers. Dances and balls on moonshiny nights. Close press of village life. Snugness.

But all the kinship I feel in life is for my native scrub. As fitted to that place as the eye "to the use of seeing." Mediterranean shore and rocky spine rising from the water. Sound and scent of those waves against the headland. Taste of the salt in the brush itself. All the kinship I have ever needed. No less real, for all that, than Mr. Gilbert White, who counts up his scores of nephews and nieces as they are added to the fold. Who knows better than most the claims of place.

I do well enough here till winter comes. An inaccurate observer would conclude that my breed might prosper in England. And yet this is merely the facsimile of a life. I am native now only to this garden. To Mr. Gilbert White's presence. Contemplating the welcome ache of this existence.

I had other expectations once. They come upon me sometimes as I dig my hybernaculum. In the rust of autumn. Mere phantoms now. Until I drift away under the snow. Find the current again.

## Timothy

I do not fret my summer days at the edge of the ha-ha. Worry how to get over the fruit-wall or around the precipice of Mr. Gilbert White's house. I never hope to be carried out of the cabbage by some willing accomplice, into the Ewell or over the sheep-down. No illusions about what lies beyond this place. Brick-walk through the wicket-gate does not lead to rough Cilicia. No retracing the path of chance.

But my motive for leaving is plain enough. Neither hunger nor love.

I wish to be out of human reach. Out from under the constant stir. Laborious turmoil of this breed. Endless bother of humans. Toil inherent in their mere existence. Dizzying inability to bask or muse.

The painstaking paradise of this garden. Adjoining fields. Plotting and measuring and planning. Cutting vistas. Raising obelisks and oil-jars. Touching up poor Hercules. Trimming hedges. Amending this bit of earth and that bit. Mining chalk to spread on the fields. Digging basins to fill with black malm. Burying rank, stiff, wheat-bearing clay under loads of ashes and manure. Under marl, lime rubbish, peat-dust, soot from the malt-house, old rotting thatch. Woolen rags to be dug into the hop-garden. Half a barrel of American gypsum on the fourth ridge of Timothy Turner's wheat.

Whole sapling-forests in transit. Cargoes of shrubs. Hither and yon. London to Selborne and back again. Perpetual traffic in slips and seeds and cuttings and roots.

Nursery Garden, late Shields. Ferne & Thatcher, Seedsmen and Netmakers at the Raven in Fleet Street. Mr. William Curtis. Mr. Philip Miller. A start from the vicarage. Annuals, bulbs, and endive from Daniel Wheeler. Bulbous roots, lifted and hung in a paper bag in the lumber-garret.

Hot-beds in late winter. Cart-loads of steaming manure. Stercoraceous heaps. Cucumber frames and hand-glasses and stowing them away again. Memorandum on their whereabouts. The pegs that hold the frames together. Planting asparagus and grubbing it up. Picking caterpillars off the Savoys. Play of the water-engine over the vegetable rows in droughty weeks. Weeding and hoeing. Tacking and pruning. Raking and mowing. Sweeping and edging. Coming and going. Annual recurrence of Goody Hammond, regular as a swift. Bleeding with pity as always. Fastidiousness. Preparation. Harvest.

On the street the clangor of the blacksmith's hammer. Above the Plestor the bells of St. Mary's. Bellowing of herded kine in the fields at weaning. Cry of the hop-poles in the spring wind. Uproar of the cattle-fair and honey-market. Combs from upland bee-gardens sold from a cart. Cranberries, whortleberries, herring, and mackerel hawked at the door. Shouts of men and boys from the cricketing-place cut by the curate nearly forty years ago. Sudden crowd in the street. Tumult of spectacle and entertainment. Ass-races. Toad-eating quack. Country people staring in wonder. Porker to be shot for in the Christmas season. Boar-pigs to be bowled for. Farmering to be played at for a good watch of one guinea value.

This is the headache that gratifies humans so. Contagion of their company. Stew they frolic in. I have no part in it. Want none.

Not just the fracas, the roiling of their presence. Only a human could love the order of this garden. Laid out as carefully as the prayer-book. Profound affection for geometry. Firs in the quincunx. Vegetable indices in sharp, neat rows. Planted just so, just thus, just short of alphabetical. The eye herded down views. Decoyed into landscapes. Gaps in the hedges promptly filled. Carrots and cabbages picked to preserve the symmetry of their beds. Each blade of grass on the grass-plot cut to just the same height. Plants that play truant encouraged to do so to heighten the sense of order.

Mr. Gilbert White knows the particulars of every specimen visible from the kitchen door. From the gentle summit of Baker's Hill. He writes of trees in the outlet having overstood their time. Maples, hazels, white-thorn, laid out in walks by his father. But he is also thinking of himself. His own time nearly over-stood. Landscape of names and origins. Associations reaching back to his grandfather's days and beyond. Memory of Man, impossibly short.

But I wish to live in the ancient disorder of nature again. Where everything grows according to its kind. As it will or won't, without the work of human hands. Arising from the natural ground, as Mr. Gilbert White calls it. Infinitely subtler order lying outside this garden. Nearly out of the reach of human memory. Beyond mead and Hanger and sheep-walk. Beyond Ewell-close and litton-close. If only in some overlooked interstice of the parish. No telling how far away true wildness lies. Perhaps none to be found short of cross-ing those seas again.

"All nature is so full," Mr. Gilbert White writes, "that that district produces the greatest variety which is the most examined."

True enough. But that greatest variety exists even if not examined. Begins to diminish when examiners settle down in the district. Raise their walls. Bound their fields. Improve their husbandry. Set the way-menders to working the roads.

The old wonder I felt crossing into the order of that ancient city. Out of the scrub and onto those mosaic floors. Nakedness I felt for once. My presence echoing off those broken walls. Like walking on the wave-surface of the sea. Graces beneath my feet. Hermes. Nike. Feeling that I was being watched from below. From above. From every angle. From past and future. Feeling that I was falling.

To break the spell I simply stepped back into the scrub. Out of the human and into the clover. Onto the scree. Suddenly myself again.

To live in the streets the humans had abandoned. To abandon them myself whenever I liked. Harsh outlines, painful geometries of the city, softened by decay. Whorled lines of brush capping the walls as if to hide the city from discovery by sea. Walls sinking into the scrub. As if the thatch of Selborne had taken root and sent up seed-head. Whole village bedaubed by martins and swallows in their building until Selborne is more hirundine than human. Not a straight line left.

I wish to live again in a place that is not a map of the gardener's mind. Book of nature, as humans love to think of it. But where I wish to live is not a book at all. Not an argument for the being and attributes of an unnecessary god. Not a theorem, hypothesis, or demonstration. Merely itself.

· · · · · ⌒

**O**f the eggs laid alongside mine in the nest, how many ever hatched? And of those hatchlings how many still live? How did it come about that I have survived all these years? And survived, thus long, this strange dislocation? Out of such questions, the gods are made.

But it is only a matter of chance. Long odds. Doze elsewhere on that one day, fifty-three years ago, and the sea might still roll to a stop at my feet. Hatched in the rubble of an ancient country. Lodged—abandoned—in the oat-green glory of this all-too-human place. This alien abundance. How one life led to another there is no explaining. No *why* to be reasoned out.

Mediterranean skies over Selborne now and then. Glow

of a southern sea. But the Hampshire sky staggers me now with loveliness. Creeping fogs in the pastures. Gossamer on the stubbles. The parish rings with light. Whole being of the world distilled into a moment. When everything I know and remember seems to surround me at once, embodied in this tangible earth.

I think of those who have not lived to see what I have seen. Wonder that only I, of all my race, should be present here to notice. Weltering flocks on wing overhead. Aurora dimming the northern stars. But the first condition of beauty is survival.

Mr. Gilbert White outlasts his younger brothers. Mr. John White and Mr. Henry White. Four other siblings lost in infancy or youth. Parents long dead. Mrs. Rebecca Snooke. Poor dear niece, Mrs. Brown, dies in childbirth. One by one, the neighbors fall away. Mr. Richard Yalden. Reverend Andrew Etty. Burbeys and Lassams. Beachers and Berrimans. Dame Turner. Widow Othen in her old age. Warwick, infant son of Mr. and Mrs. George Smith. The curate chronicles them out of existence as they go. Signs the register. Leads the prayer. Lets the spade resume its work.

Hopes to survive himself in some supernal city. The hope of all his little flock. As vain, as unnecessary, as the wishes of a garden-tortoise half a lifetime away from her natural home.

Today. Cold dew, louring clouds. Warming, softening.

# Timothy

Iron going out of the ground at last. Sun less reluctant. Summer promising and overdue. Men wash their sheep. One by one. Ready the fleece for shearing. Ewes and wethers flow past dogs and men in the fields. Flat nasal peals shoal over the parish. Whistles of men. The very voice of mid-June.

Mr. Gilbert White. In his bed-shirt at the window above the kitchen. There for only a moment a few days past. Face washed by illness. Dimmed by bright clouds mirroring across the glass. Last in this garden several days ago. Walking among the dames violets. The ten-weeks stocks. Cutting four cucumbers. How much of his life has he devoted to that fruit!

His plans are laid. To lie in his bed a little longer. To be borne from St. Mary's by six day-laboring men with families to raise. Six shillings each for a short morning's service.

To be placed in a grave in the natural ground in the shade of the church-walls. Simple stone. "G. W." and the numeral of a day in June in the human year 1793. As plain as his initials set into the fruit-wall above me. By hop-picking time, grass will stir on his grave, thick in the wind. As if he had always lain there. Interred, like his father, "with as little show and expense as may be and without any monument, not desiring to have my name recorded save in the Book of Life."

For now, there is all the doctoring to be got through. Back and forth of William Web, surgeon of Alton. Journey in the morning. Journey in the evening. Duly receipted. Eight days end on end. With him come his wares, his potions, his useless knowledge. Alkaline mixtures, acid mixtures. Lavender water and laudanum. Draughts, emulsions, ointments, boluses. Fomentations, nestringents, anodynes. Gum Arabic. Burnt hartshorn. Spirit of niter. Enough to kill a strapping young yeoman. Patient forced to comfort the doctor more than once. To deny his pain and acknowledge his hopes, if not for this world.

Result: bill for nine pounds, eight shillings, tuppence. Fee to Dr. Littlehaler included. Horses and a post-boy express that final morning. To Salisbury for Mr. John White, the former Gibraltar Jack. His bride of this year, late Miss Louisa Neave, making the last of the curate's nephews and nieces, numbering sixty-two.

The naturalist in Mr. Gilbert White will watch as closely as the cleric in him for the approach of that interesting moment. Quiet dissolution of self. Mrs. John White at his bedside. Warm, strong hands on his. And Thomas. Man, servant, and gardener to him these forty years. Standing beside the window. Looking now at the garden and the Great Mead and Hanger beyond it. Now at the form in the bed. Outside, the whetting of a mower's scythe on an early, dewy morning. Sound his master rejoiced in.

In their presence, the answer to one of Mr. Gilbert White's lifelong questions comes upon him. Merely human at last. One earthly parish only.

# Timothy

Most years the bees have swarmed by now. Dark tempest outside the bee-stall, rising in uproar before settling in the Balm of Gilead. Long beard of bees dangling from a bough. The generations come and go quickly this time of year. One after another. Bright new sisters clambering over the cells. Spilling from the hive and into the sky, as if sucked from the opening. Droning over the entire garden. Over the Great Mead and into the uplands. Profuse over the blossoms of this parish.

This year the swarms come late. Hirundines slow in building and breeding. Deterred by a summer so cold and dry. Wells sinking. Kingsley mill failing. No grass among farmers on the sands. Ground sadly burnt-up. No season like it since 1765.

"Hollow wind," Mr. Gilbert White wrote all those years ago. Man of forty-five at the time. "I do not remember my Garden to be so totally overcome with heat & dryness so soon in the Year." Ten weeks' drought, till broken by a noble rain in early July.

Even now the weather of this present June improves. Yet improves unrecorded. Weather-glass wavers, unattended. Thermometer rises, unacknowledged. Rain-gauge spills over with the water of several showers. No one brings the balance forward.

Thomas feels the blush of fog over the garden as he

walks toward the brew-house through the morning darkness. Mrs. John White welcomes the ripening sun, even as
she prepares to begin another life. The villagers notice what
they have always noticed. They speak the words to each
other. "Sun," "showers," "sweet even," "gleams." But no one
troubles to write them down. System set aside in this place.
Present vanishes outright without leaving a trace.

Wind on the fifteenth of June 1793? From the northeast
veering to the southwest. Matter of record. Wind on the six-
teenth? No one will ever know who did not live through it.

And I will go unweighed this autumn. Experiment over.
Novelty of that ceremony long since worn off in the village. Old customer by now in Mr. Jack Burbey's shop. Mrs.
Elizabeth Burbey, his wife, does the weighing. Cool hands.
Her husband ages too. At rising this year I weigh six pounds
five and a half ounces. No particular notice of my six ounces
lost since April last. Even the naturalist makes no mention
of it. Merely a fact in a world of facts.

I notice. I am slowly eroding. This England is washing me
away.

Unobserved and uninscribed, like the weather. One more
winter in me. Whether it is mild or savage. Into my hybernaculum for good. Well embarked by the time the humans discover where I lie. When the snows melt. When
the nightingale sings. When swifts dash and play round the
church again.

But till I dig that last nest and snow settles over the

garden, a time remains to me. Stub of days still longer than the lives of many creatures in this parish. Substantial to me even after so many years. See the human season out once more. Sainfoin in the rick. Turnips hoeing. Chalk hauling. Fallows stirring against the coming year. Hops in the kiln. Barley malting. Pigs in the beech-mast and acorns. The drawing and stacking of turnips.

Parlor-fire lit. Fine autumnal tinges. Leaves falling fast. Maple hedges aglow in the last sun of afternoon. Russets and dearlings hang fast in the trees. Swan's-egg and Chaumontel and Virgoleuse pears. Twilight seems to ripen them. Rush-lights begin to flicker around the village. As pale as the first stars overhead.

I dig and dig. Settle the dirt on my shell. As deep as I can go into the warmth of earth. Carefully overlaid with autumn's debris. Anchored. Immured. Landlocked. Becalmed and buoyed in the doldrums of Selborne.

# Historical Note

This is a true story. Timothy's shell is preserved in the Natural History Museum in London. Scientists in the nineteenth century determined from the shape of the shell that Timothy was indeed female. A modern scientist has confirmed that fact and demonstrated that Timothy came from a subspecies of tortoise whose native home is the central Mediterranean coast of Turkey.

The topography around Gilbert White's house and the village of Selborne itself has changed very little over the years. Gilbert White kept a spare but detailed natural history journal for most of his adult life. He also saved many of his household receipts, which are in the Houghton Library at Harvard University. His letters were collected more than a century ago, and a new edition is long overdue. One or two of his sermons have been published; manuscripts of others are also at Harvard. And, of course, there is White's great work, *The Natural History and Antiquities of Selborne*, which was published in early 1789 and has now gone out of print for the first time in more than two hundred years. Using these works, and much research besides, I have tried to make this portrait of Selborne and the life around it as accurate as possible. Timothy's language and opinions are her own, except where she borrows—silently—from the quiet poetry of Gilbert White's journals.

# Glossary

> "But without a glossary how should men know what the *lorum* of a Bird is!"
>
> Gilbert White to John White, 31 October 1777

**After-grass:** the grass in hay-fields after the hay has been cut.

**Alice Holt:** a forest near Selborne. Lord Stawel lived in the great lodge.

**Alton:** a nearby town.

**Anathoth:** a place of echoes; see commentary on Isaiah 10:30. "This village is another *Anathoth*, a place of *responses* or *echoes*," NHS.

**Arum dracunculus:** the dragon plant, *Dracunculus vulgaris*.

**Autopsia:** literally, seeing for oneself. The evidence obtained by doing so.

**Bait:** "To stop at an inn, orig. to feed the horses, but later also to rest and refresh themselves; hence, to make a brief stay or sojourn," OED.

**Baker's Hill:** a gently rising garden, about an acre in extent, behind Gilbert White's house.

**Balk:** the ridge left between two furrows.

**Balm of Gilead tree:** balsam fir, *Abies balsamea*.

**Barrow-hog:** a castrated male hog.

**Besom:** a broom.

**Billet, beech-billet:** a stick of wood, firewood.

# Glossary

**Birdlime:** a sticky substance for catching birds—and wasps.

**Bittern:** a heron-like bird, *Botaurus stellaris*. "These birds are very seldom seen in this district, & are probably driven from their watery haunts by the great floods, & obliged to betake themselves to the uplands," *Journals*, 14 January 1774.

**Black-cap:** a warbler, *Sylvia atricapilla*. "When that bird sits calmly and engages in song in earnest, he pours forth very sweet, but inward melody, and expresses great variety of soft and gentle modulations, superior perhaps to those of any of our warblers, the nightingale excepted," NHS.

**Blains:** swellings, sores, blisters.

**Blattae:** cockroaches.

**Blue rag:** rag is a kind of stone that breaks up into flat pieces. The blue rags of Selborne, White noted, "are excellent for pitching of stables, paths and courts, and for building of dry walls against banks; a valuable species of fencing, much in use in this village, and for mending of roads," NHS.

**Blue titmouse:** a bird, the blue tit, *Parus caeruleus*. "The blue *titmouse*, or *nun*, is a great frequenter of houses, and a general devourer. Beside insects, it is very fond of flesh; for it frequently picks bones on dunghills: it is a vast admirer of suet, and haunts butchers' shops," NHS.

**Borecole:** kale.

**Bostal:** a diagonal path rising up the face of the Hanger. It was dug in 1780 and is 414 yards long.

**Brighthelmstone:** now known as Brighton.

**Buckram:** "A kind of coarse linen or cloth stiffened with gum or paste," OED.

**Bullfinch:** small bird with a pinkish-red breast and a black cap, *Pyrrhula pyrrhula*. "Bulfinches, when fed on hempseed, often become wholly black," NHS.

**Butcher-bird:** the red-backed shrike, *Lanius collurio*. "The next bird that I procured (on the 21st of May) was a male red-backed butcher bird, *lanius collurio*. My neighbour, who shot it, says that it might easily have escaped his notice, had not the outcries and chattering of the white-throats and other small birds drawn his attention to the bush where it was: its craw was filled with the legs and wings of beetles," NHS.

**Caique:** a Turkish boat or skiff.

**Calipash:** the green, edible fat just below a turtle's carapace.

**Calipee:** the edible "yellowish gelatinous substance" (OED) just inside a turtle's plastron.

**Cambric:** fine white linen, often used in handkerchiefs.

**Camlet:** a rich fabric, something like camel hair.

**Candlemas:** 2 February.

**Caponize:** to castrate a young rooster.

**Caprimulgus:** a synonym for the nightjar, *Caprimulgus europaeus*.

**Carapace:** shell.

**Chafer:** A large beetle, the common cockchafer, *Melolontha melolontha*. "The crows, rooks, & daws in great numbers continue to devour the chafers on the hanger. Was it not for those birds chafers would destroy everything," *Journals*, 28 May 1774.

**Chaumontel:** a variety of pear.

**Chichester:** port city south of Selborne.

**Chiffchaff:** a small warbler, *Phylloscopus collybita*. "The uncrested wren, the smallest species, called in this place the Chif-chaf, is very loud in the Lythe. This is the earliest summer-bird of passage, & the harbinger of spring. It has only two piercing notes," *Journals*, 18 March 1780.

**Church-close:** the enclosure surrounding a churchyard.

**Churn-owl:** a synonym for the nightjar, *Caprimulgus europaeus*.

**Cilicia:** Rough Cilicia is the ancient name of a part of Turkey, including the region where the Tarsus Mountains meet the sea. Timothy would have come from the eastern slopes of those mountains, near the coastal Byzantine ruin called Anemurium. Her species lives there still.

**Cleft-wood:** split wood.

**Close-stool:** a small stool that encloses a chamber-pot.

**Coal-mouse:** coal tit, a small, chickadee-like bird, *Parus ater*. "Cole-mouse roosts in the eaves of a thatched house," *Journals*, 2 December 1771.

**Cockerel:** a young rooster.

**Common:** "A common land or estate; the undivided land belonging to the members of a local community as a whole. Hence, often, the patch of unenclosed or 'waste' land which remains to represent that," OED.

**Compasses, The:** the inn at Selborne.

**Cooperage:** the making of casks and barrels, the products of the cooper's trade.

**Coppice:** a small wood of trees that regrow quickly when cut, usually ash, chestnut, or hazel. To coppice is to cut such trees. A coppice provides fuel, garden-rods, hops-poles, etc.

**Corn:** wheat.

**Coss lettuce:** an upright, open lettuce.

**Cross-bill:** common crossbill, *Loxia curvirostra*. "About Midsummer a flight of *cross-bills* comes to the pine-groves about [Mrs. Snooke's] house, but never makes any long stay," NHS.

**Crown-imperial:** a flower, *Fritillaria imperialis*.

**Curate:** a clergyman who serves in place of the parish vicar. Gilbert White served as the curate of Selborne three times, including most of the last decade of his life, but he was never its vicar.

**Daffy-down-dilly:** daffodil.

**Dames violet:** a flower, dame's rocket, *Hesperis matronalis*.

**Daw:** a bird, the jackdaw, *Corvus monedula*. "Crows and *daws* swagger in their walk," NHS.

**Deal:** pine board.

**Dearling:** a variety of apple.

**Deer-cart:** "the covered cart in which a tame stag to be hunted is carried to the meet," OED.

**Dimity:** "A stout cotton fabric, woven with raised stripes or fancy figures," OED.

**Dishabille:** careless dress.

**Dissenters:** Protestants who did not belong to the Church of England.

**Dorton:** a wooded common on the northeast side of Selborne street. The soil there, a black malm, is much richer than the heavy clay soil on the southwest side, where Gilbert White's house—called the Wakes—still stands.

**Doublet:** a close-fitting shirt or jacket.

**Duodecimo:** a small printed book.

**Dutch-currant tree:** a variety of currant.

**Dutch lettuce:** hardy winter lettuce.

**Eve-jar:** a synonym for the nightjar, *Caprimulgus europaeus*.

**Ewe:** a female sheep.

**Ewell, Ewel:** a strip of fields and enclosures between the houses on the south side of Gracious Street and the Hanger. Gilbert White's outlet—his back garden—connected to the Ewell.

**Fane:** a weathercock.

**Faringdon:** a neighboring parish.

**Fern-owl:** a synonym for the nightjar, *Caprimulgus europaeus*.

**Fire-drake:** a dragon.

**Five November:** Guy Fawkes Day, commemorating the discovery of a plot to blow up Parliament and King James I in 1605. Celebrated with fireworks.

# Glossary

**Flitch:** a side of bacon.

**Florence-oil:** olive oil.

**Flycatcher:** a phoebe-like bird now called the spotted flycatcher, *Muscicapa striata*. "The flycatcher is a very harmless, & honest bird, medling with nothing but insects," *Journals*, 4 July 1776.

**Freehold:** property owned outright.

**Fustian:** "A kind of coarse cloth made of cotton and flax," OED.

**Gilt:** a young female pig.

**Glass:** barometer.

**Glebe-close:** a glebe is a "portion of land assigned to a clergyman as part of his benefice," OED.

**Glow-worm:** *Lampyris noctiluca*, a beetle. The end of the adult female's abdomen lights up like a firefly's.

**Goatsucker:** a synonym for the nightjar, *Caprimulgus europaeus*.

**Goleigh Wood:** a wood in the neighboring parish of East Tisted.

**Goodwoman:** a title, often abbreviated "Goody," for a married woman "in humble life," OED.

**Goose-hatch:** a goose gate, I presume.

**Goree:** an island near Senegal.

**Gossamer:** "The remark that I shall make on these cobweb-like appearances, called *gossamer*, is, that, strange and superstitious as the notions about them were formerly, nobody in these days doubts but that they are the real production of small spiders, which swarm in the fields in fine weather in autumn, and have a power of shooting out webs from their tails so as to render themselves buoyant, and lighter than air," NHS.

**Gracious Street:** a street that curves to the southwest and west off Selborne street next to Gilbert White's house.

**Grasshopper lark:** the grasshopper warbler, *Locustella naevia*. "The grasshopper-lark chirps all night in the height of summer," NHS.

**Greenfinch:** a bird, *Carduelis chloris*. "The cock green-finch begins to toy, & hang about on the wing in a very peculiar manner. These gestures proceed from amorous propensities," *Journals*, 24 April 1777.

**Green goose:** a young goose.

**Guinea:** a gold coin worth twenty-one shillings, one shilling more than a pound.

**Ha-ha:** a sunken fence, faced, in this case, with brick. Gilbert White built one of the first ones in England, and it is still standing. From his house, the ha-ha is invisible, but from the fields beyond it forms an effective barrier against grazing animals. "Because we call this creature an abject reptile, we are too apt to undervalue his abilities, and depreciate his powers of instinct. Yet he is, as Mr. *Pope* says of his lord,—'Much too wise to walk into a well:' and has so much discernment as not to fall down an haha; but to stop and withdraw from the brink with the readiest precaution," NHS.

**Hand-glass:** a glass bell placed over young plants to protect them from cold; a cloche.

**Hanger:** Behind Gilbert White's house, and running parallel to Selborne's main street, is what White called "a vast hill of chalk, rising three hundred feet above the village." The northern side of that hill, facing White's house, is covered by "a long hanging wood called The Hanger. The covert of this eminence is altogether beech, the most lovely of all forest trees, whether we consider its smooth rind or bark, its glossy foliage, or graceful pendulous boughs," NHS.

**Hartshorn:** a type of smelling salts.

**Haw:** fruit of the hawthorn.

**Hawksbill:** a now-endangered sea turtle, *Eretmochelys imbricata*, whose shell was prized for making tortoise-shell objects.

**Hecatomb:** "A great public sacrifice (properly of a hundred oxen) among the ancient Greeks and Romans, and hence extended to the religious sacrifices of other nations," OED.

**Hepatica:** a flower, perhaps *Hepatica triloba*.

**Hesperian Hercules:** a board-statue representing Hercules while performing his Hesperian labors, perhaps holding the golden apples of the Hesperides.

**Hirundine:** now, pertaining to swallows. Gilbert White used the word to include swallows, swifts, and martins.

**Hitt's book on wall fruit:** Thomas Hitt's A *Treatise of Fruit Trees*, 1755.

**Holland:** a linen fabric.

**Honey-buzzard:** *Pernis apivoris*. "A pair of honey-buzzards, & a pair of wind-hovers appear to have young in the hanger. The honey-buzzard is a fine hawk, & skims about in a majestic manner," *Journals*, 12 September 1787.

**Hoopoe:** a thrush-sized crested bird, *Upupa epops*, an occasional visitor to England. "The most unusual birds I ever observed in these parts were a pair of *hoopoes* (*upupa*) which came several years ago in the summer, and frequented an ornamented piece of ground, which joins to my garden, for some weeks. They used to march about in a stately manner, feeding in the walks, many times in the day; and seemed disposed to breed in my outlet; but were frightened and persecuted by idle boys, who would never let them be at rest," NHS.

**Hops:** a climbing, vining plant, *Humulus lupulus*, whose dried flowers are used in brewing beer. In Gilbert White's day, Selborne had many hop-gardens, where hops grew on chestnut poles. "Brewed half an Hogsh: of strong-beer with 6 Bushels of Rich: Knight's malt, & two pounds & three quarters of good Hops. The water was from the well," *Journals*, 1 March 1766.

**Huckaback:** "a stout linen fabric," OED. Coarse, for toweling.

**Hybernaculum Hibernacula** (plural): "The winter quarters or place of retirement of a hibernating animal," OED.

**Isinglass:** mica.

**Lammas, lammas-growth:** Lammas is the first of August. Lammas-growth is a late-summer growth.

**Land-rail:** Gilbert White means the corncrake, *Crex crex*, a secretive bird. "I have often heard them cry, Crex, Crex," *Journals*, 3 October 1789.

**Larker:** a person who nets larks.

**Lavant:** a land-spring, a spontaneous spring of water that appears after heavy rains. The word was local to Selborne.

**Leaseholder:** a person who holds property by lease.

**Lime tree:** *Tilia europaeus*, known in America as the linden tree.

**Linnaean system:** the binomial system of scientific nomenclature developed by Linnaeus in the mid-eighteenth century.

**Litton-close:** a churchyard close, or enclosure.

**Lodge** (verb): wheat that has lodged has been beaten down by wind or rain.

**Loggerhead:** a now-endangered sea turtle, *Caretta caretta*, which nests, among other places, on the Mediterranean coast of Turkey, where Timothy lived before being carried to England.

**Long-legged plover:** the black-winged stilt, *Himantopus himantopus*. "These are the most rare of all British birds. Their legs are marvellously long for the bulk of their bodies. To be in proportion of weight for inches the legs of the Flamingo should be more than 10 feet in length," *Journals*, 28 April 1779.

**Lop and top:** the branches trimmed from trees cut for timber. In 1784, Lord Stawel had a large number of trees cut down in the Holt forest. "He lays claim also to the lop and top: but the poor of the parishes of *Binsted* and *Frinsham*, *Bentley* and *Kingsley*, assert that it belongs to them; and, assembling in a riotous manner, have actually taken it all away," NHS.

**Lorum:** the space between the eye and the bill of a bird.

**Lythe:** (pronounced "lith"): "a steep abrupt pasture field," NHS. Just north of Selborne's village street lies the Short Lythe and the Long Lythe.

**Magdalen College:** the Oxford College that appointed the vicar of Selborne and cut the beeches on the Hanger.

**Malm:** "A warm forward, crumbling mould, called *black malm*, which seems highly saturated with vegetable and animal manure," NHS. White also refers to "white malm," which the OED defines as "a greyish-white calcareous sandstone."

**Malt, malting, maltster:** When barley, a grain, is allowed to germinate slightly and is then dried it has been malted. Malted barley is a staple, with hops, of brewing.

**Marl:** a loose earth deposit, part clay, part calcium carbonate, used to enrich soil.

**Martin:** usually Gilbert White means the house-martin, *Delicon urbica*. "Martins are seldom seen at any distance from neighbourhoods. They feed over waters or under the shelter of an hanging wood," *Journals*, 1 October 1773. He also refers to the bank martin, now called the sand martin, *Riparia riparia*.

**Marvel of Peru:** *Mirabilis jalapa*, or four o'clock.

***Merops apiaster*:** a bird, the European bee-eater.

**Merry-tree:** a wild cherry, *Prunus avium*.

**Meteor:** Gilbert White uses this word in an archaic sense, meaning "Any atmospheric or meteorological phenomenon," OED.

**Michaelmas:** 29 September.

**Milch-sow:** a sow that is lactating.

**Miller, the new edition:** In October 1753, Gilbert White bought the new edition of Philip Miller's *The Gardener's Dictionary*, perhaps the most important gardening book published in his lifetime.

**Milt:** semen of a male fish.

**Mistle thrush:** *Turdus viscivorus*. "The missel-thrush, tho' most shy in the autumn & winter, builds in my garden close to a walk where people are passing all day long," *Journals*, 16 April 1774.

**Monography:** a treatise on a single species.

**Muscadine vine:** a variety of grape.

**Necessary house:** a privy or outhouse.

**Necropolis:** a burying ground.

**Needy shop, a tortoise hung in a:** the apothecary's shop described by Romeo in *Romeo and Juliet*, Act V, scene I:

> *And in his needy shop a tortoise hung,*
> *An alligator stuff'd, and other skins*
> *Of ill-shap'd fishes.*

**Newton Valence:** a neighboring parish. Gilbert White's nephew Edmund White became vicar of Newton Valence.

**Nidification:** nest-making.

**Nightjar:** one of Gilbert White's favorite birds, *Caprimulgus europaeus*.

**Oakhanger:** a nearby village. Oakhanger stream runs in a northeasterly direction from just behind St. Mary's church in Selborne.

**Odeon:** Byzantine theater in the abandoned city of Anemurium.

**Oliphant:** elephant. This refers to the size of a sheet of paper, twenty-eight inches by twenty-three inches.

**Oriel College:** Gilbert White was a fellow of this Oxford college.

**Ostler:** stableman at an inn.

**Palmer-worm:** a caterpillar.

**Patten:** a kind of elevated wooden sandal.

**Peg-top:** a wooden top spun by a string.

**Pettichaps:** a bird, the lesser whitethroat, *Sylvia curruca*. "Restless & active like the willow-wrens, hopping from bough to bough, & examining every part for food. It also runs up the stems of the crown-imperials," *Journals*, 11 May 1782.

**Physico-theologist:** one who practices physico-theology, which is "a theology founded upon the facts of nature, and the evidences of design there found; natural theology," OED. The chief physico-theological texts are William Derham's *Physico-Theology; or, A Demonstration of the Being and Attributes of God, from His Works of Creation* (1713) and John Ray's *The Wisdom of God Manifested in the Works of Creation* (1691). To one correspondent, Gilbert White writes, in August 1792, "I concur with you most heartily in your admiration of the harmony and beauty of the works of the creation! Physico-theology is a noble study, worthy the attention of the wisest man!"

**Pinchbeck:** a cheap alloy resembling gold.

**Pink:** a flower of the *Dianthus* genus.

**Pip:** to break out of an egg.

**Pizzle:** penis.

**Plastron:** the under-shell of a tortoise.

**Plestor:** "In the centre of the village, and near the church, is a square piece of ground surrounded by houses, and vulgarly called *The Plestor*," NHS.

**Pompion:** pumpkin.

**Portland:** a kind of gray stone.

**Portmanteau horse:** pack-horse.

**Post-chaise:** "A travelling carriage, either hired from stage to stage, or drawn by horses so hired," OED. Usually yellow, closed, and intended for two to four persons.

**Pound Field:** field at the base of the Zigzag.

**Puckeridge:** a synonym for the nightjar, *Caprimulgus europaeus*.

**Quincunx:** a planting of trees in a grouping of five. Gilbert White planted a quincunx of firs on Baker's Hill.

**Redbreast:** the English robin, *Erithacus rubecula*. "The redbreast's note is very sweet, & pleasing; did it not carry with it ugly associations of ideas, & put us in mind of the approach of winter," *Journals*, 16 October 1776.

**Redstart:** a bird, *Phoenicurus phoenicurus*. "The redstart begins to sing: its note is short and imperfect, but is continued till about the middle of June," NHS.

**Redwing:** a bird, *Turdus iliacus*. "Redwings begin to appear on their winter-visit. . . . When redwings come, woodcocks are near at hand," *Journals*, 11 October 1778.

**Rick:** a stack of hay, etc., usually thatched.

**Ringmer:** the Sussex town where Mrs. Rebecca Snooke lived, some eighty miles east of Selborne.

**Ring ousel:** a bird, *Turdus torquatus*. "In autumn they feed on haws and yew-berries, and in the spring on ivy-berries. I dressed one of these birds, and found it juicy and well-flavoured. It is remarkable that they make but a few days stay in their spring visit, but rest near a fortnight at *Michaelmas*," NHS.

**Rock-water:** spring water.

**Rook:** a crow-like bird, *Corvus frugilegus*. "Rooks visit their nest-trees every morning just at the dawn of the day, being preceded a few minutes by a flight of daws: & again about sunset. At the close of day they retire into deep woods to roost," *Journals*, 12 December 1773.

**Rook-worm:** the larva of a chafer.

**Runnel:** a small stream.

**Rush, rush-light:** a pithy, straight-stemmed plant, the "common soft rush, which is to be found in most moist pastures, by the sides of streams, and under hedges," NHS. Rushes were used to tie hops to their poles. When soaked, stripped, dried, and dipped in scalding fat, they burn with "a good clear light," NHS.

**Russet:** a variety of apple.

**Sainfoin:** a forage and hay crop, *Onobrychis viciifolia*.

**Savoy:** a variety of cabbage.

**Scummings:** skimmings.

# Glossary

**Scute:** one of the plates that makes up the shell of a tortoise.

**Seedlap:** seedlip, a basket for carrying seed that will be hand-sown.

**Shalloon:** a material for linings.

**Shambles:** a place where animals are killed for meat.

**Sheep-down:** "The down, or sheep-walk, is a pleasing park-like spot, of about one mile by half that space, jutting out on the verge of the hill-country, where it begins to break down into the plains, and commanding a very engaging view, being an assemblage of hill, dale, wood-lands, heath, and water," NHS. The sheep-down was on top of the Hanger.

**Silk-wood:** "Stalks of the *polytrichum commune*, or *great golden maiden-hair*," NHS.

**Smock-frock:** a loose frock, worn by farmers and laborers.

**Snipe:** a bird, *Gallinago gallinago*. "Snipes play over the moors, piping, & humming. They always hum as they are descending," *Journals*, 4 June 1768.

**Sough:** "To make a rushing, rustling, or murmuring sound," OED.

**Sowthistle:** a milky thistle of the *Sonchus* genus, probably the smooth sowthistle, *Sonchus oleraceus*. Writing of Timothy, Gilbert White says, "Milky plants, such as lettuces, dandelions, sow-thistles, are its favourite dish," NHS.

**Sparrow's hanger:** a nearby wood that belonged to Gilbert White.

**Speaking-trumpet:** an ear trumpet.

**Squab-young:** a young bird still in the nest.

**Stercoraceous:** "Consisting of, containing, or pertaining to feces," OED. The word appears, famously, in William Cowper's poem "The Task," in reference to preparing a hot-bed for cucumbers.

**Stickleback:** a small fish, *Gasterosteus aculeatus*.

**Stoat:** an ermine, *Mustela erminea*, in its brown summer phase.

**Stock, ten-weeks stocks:** a flower, *Matthiola incana* var. *annua*.

**Stone-curlew:** a bird, *Burhinus oedicnemus.* "That noise in the air of some thing passing quick over our heads after it becomes dark, & which we found last year proceeded from the Stone-curlew, has now been heard for a week or more," *Journals*, 20 March 1790.

**Storm-cock:** synonym for the mistle thrush, *Turdus viscivorus.*

**Stoup:** a bucket; also a "vessel to contain holy-water, usu. a stone basin set in or against the wall of the church-porch, or within the church close to the entrance-door," OED.

**Straddle-bob:** White seems to mean a sprawling creature. "The great straddle-bob, Orion, that in the winter seems to bestride my brew-house, is seen now descending of an evening, on one side foremost, behind the hanger," Gilbert White to Samuel Barker, 17 April 1786.

**Stubbles:** fields after grain has been harvested.

**Stuff:** "a woollen fabric," OED.

**Summer-cock:** a measure of hay that has been gathered, part of a rick.

**Surplice:** a clergyman's outer vestment, usually of white linen.

**Swan's-egg:** a variety of pear.

**Sycamore:** White means the sycamore maple, *Acer pseudoplatanus*, not the American sycamore, *Platanus occidentalis.*

**Taw:** "A large choice or fancy marble, often streaked or variegated, being that with which the player shoots," OED.

**Timotheus:** Gilbert White is quoting from "Alexander's Feast," by John Dryden.

**Titlark:** White's name for what are now two different bird species; the meadow pipit, *Anthus pratensis*, and the tree pipit, *Anthus trivialis.* "The titlark, a sweet songster, not only sings flying in its descent, & on trees; but also on the ground, as it walks about feeding in pastures," *Journals*, 21 April 1773.

# Glossary

**Titmouse:** Now called the marsh tit, *Parus palustris*. "The titmouse, which early in *February* begins to make two quaint notes, like the whetting of a saw, is the marsh titmouse," NHS.

**"Tityre, tu patulae recubans . . .":** The Whites are shouting out the apt first words of the opening line of Virgil's first *Eclogue*, "*Tityre, tu patulae recubans sub tegmine fagi,*" which has been translated by Seamus Heaney as: "Tityrus, there you are, stretched out in the shade of the broad beech."

**Toadflax:** ivy-leaved toadflax, *Cymbalaria muralis*.

**Tow:** fiber of flax, hemp, or jute.

**Treacle:** molasses.

**Trinity:** the Sunday after Pentecost, or the eighth Sunday after Easter.

**Tun:** to store in a cask.

**Tup:** a male sheep, a ram.

**Turnip:** growing turnips for feeding sheep became widespread in England in the mid-eighteenth century.

**Umbrageous:** shaded, shadowy.

**Vallisneria:** a genus that includes several mosses and aquatic plants.

**Vespa:** a genus that includes hornets.

**Vicar:** generally, in the Church of England, the priest who is incumbent in a parish. The vicar sometimes hires a curate, like Gilbert White, to perform his duties for him.

**Virgoleuse:** a variety of pear.

**Virtù:** broadly, a love of learning and art. White, for instance, talks about searching for Roman coins in the bed of Wolmer pond during two dry years in the early 1740s. "There was not much *virtù* stirring at that time in this neighbourhood," NHS.

**Vox humana:** an organ stop, meant to approximate the sound of a human voice.

**Wagtail:** a bird. The gray wagtail is *Motacilla cinerea*. The white wag-tail is now called the pied wagtail, *Motacilla alba*. "While the cows are feeding in moist low pastures, broods of wagtails, white & grey, run picking round them close up to their noses, & under their very bellies," *Journals*, 26 August 1776.

**Warren:** "A piece of land appropriated to the breeding of rabbits (formerly also of hares)," OED.

**Water-eft:** a type of newt.

**Water-engine:** White used a barrel on wheels to water his gardens.

**Wether:** a castrated male sheep.

**Weyhill Fair:** a celebrated fair for selling hops. It occurred at the beginning of October.

**Wheatear:** small ground-dwelling bird, *Oenanthe oenanthe*. "I saw a few wheatears (birds) on the Sussex down as I came along. Vast quantities are caught by the shepherds in the season," *Journals*, 20 September 1765.

**Windhover:** synonym for the European kestrel, *Falco tinnunculus*. "The *kestrel*, or *wind-hover*, has a peculiar mode of hanging in the air in one place, his wings all the while being briskly agitated," NHS.

**Wood-owl:** tawny owl, *Strix aluco*. "Brown wood-owls come down from the hanger in the dusk of the evening, & sit hooting all night on my wall-nut trees. Their note is like a fine *vox humana*, & very tuneable," *Journals*, 2 February 1787.

**Wry-neck:** small, sparrow-like bird, *Jynx torquilla*. White also calls this the "smallest willow-wren." One of the first of the summer birds of passage to arrive in Selborne.

**Yew-berries:** these are poisonous.

**Zigzag:** a steep path that zigzags back and forth up the face of the Hanger. It is 426 yards long, according to Gilbert White's measurement.

# Glossary

## Abbreviations:

OED     *The Oxford English Dictionary*

NHS     *The Natural History and Antiquities of Selborne*, 1789

Letters     *The Life and Letters of Gilbert White of Selborne*, by Rashleigh Holt-White (London: John Murray, 1901). Two volumes.

Journals     *The Journals of Gilbert White*, edited by Francesca Greenoak and Richard Mabey (London: Century, 1986–1989). Three volumes. I am indebted, as every student of Gilbert White must be, to the commentary and identifications provided by Ms. Greenoak and Mr. Mabey.

# Acknowledgments

This book could not have been written without the help—which I gratefully acknowledge—of the following people: William Stoneman and the staff of the Houghton Library, Harvard University; Maria Newbery and the staff of the Gilbert White House in Selborne; Beatrice Rezzori and the Santa Maddalena Foundation; and Sharon Dynak and the Ucross Foundation. I received indispensable assistance on the subject of Timothy's species and origins from Dr. Jarmo Perälä.

This book was made possible by the generosity of Gail Collins, who knows how hard it is to write a book in a world of editorial duties; by the kindness, patience, and encouragement of my editor, Dan Frank; and by the long-standing friendship and indispensable counsel of my agent, Flip Brophy.

My inexpressible debt to my wife is acknowledged in the dedication to this book.

## A Note About the Author

Verlyn Klinkenborg is the author of *Making Hay*, *The Rural Life*, and *The Last Fine Time*. A member of the editorial board of *The New York Times*, Klinkenborg lives with his wife on a small farm in upstate New York.

# A Note on the Type

This book was set in Novarese, one of many typefaces designed by Aldo Novarese (1920–1995). Novarese worked for the renowned Nebiolo foundry in Turin from 1936 to 1938, and returned there after World War II, leaving in 1975 to work on his own as a type designer.

Composed by Stratford Publishing Services,
Brattleboro, Vermont

Printed and bound by R. R. Donnelley & Sons,
Harrisonburg, Virginia

Designed by Anthea Lingeman